NDY KORNER STORE

NELSON CENTRAL

FOOD CENTRAL

Stories & Recipes from the heart of Nelson

Published by the Nelson Central School Community Group

DEDICATION

This book is dedicated to everyone who has ever given their time and energy to community projects and to children, who we hope will inherit the pleasures of creating and appreciating good food.

Published in 2012 by Nelson Central School Community Group
Nelson Central School
70 Nile Street
Nelson, New Zealand

Design by Chris Chisnall, OneCC Creative

ISBN 978-0-473-22004-4

CONTENTS

Snacks & Sides

THE MAIN EVENT

Sweet Treats

BUSKERBURGO
ROAD
CLOSED

ACKNOWLEDGEMENTS

This project would not have been possible without the talents of parents in our school and dedication from people in the wider community. Thanks firstly to Kathryn Robertson, Susannah Roddick and the Nelson Central School Community Group, who gathered us together and launched us into cookbook mode. Thanks to Alex Chisnall and Gill Rowe who, having done it before, said it was worth the effort and joined Choi Fu to help with the recipe content. Thank you to everyone who has shared recipes and stories, some of which have never been written down or shared before. In particular, thanks to those of you who, just when you thought you had done your bit, kindly prepared your recipes for photographing. Huge thanks to Sue McNulty from Broccoli Row, who gave up her Sunday and opened her café for our food shoot, helped us with food styling, made us coffees and kept smiling as kids scooted in and out of the café to consume the next round of food as it was photographed.

Many thanks to Sally O'Neill for her sensitive editing and to Suzanne Thompson and Ralph Dickson for going through the recipes with eagle eyes and practical suggestions. Thanks also to our proofreaders, including David and Frances Rae, for your attention to detail.

On a personal note, I thank my mother, Anna who came for a holiday but ended up cooking and editing. My family have given up the computer for months but are grateful that I have learned how to use the iMac better. Meanwhile they have developed their cooking skills and refined their tastebuds trying the recipes!

Thank you to Phillipa Pattison and the team at MediaWorks Nelson for their enthusiasm and support in letting the Nelson community know about *Food Central*. Thanks also to the group of young artists, who, inspired by Lori Davis, thoughtfully created illustrations for us.

We are very grateful for the expertise of professional photographers David Chadwick, Kirsten Revell and Virginia Woolf who so willingly gave their time, as well as Carly Ave, Chris Chisnall and others who supplied additional images. We have also been exceptionally fortunate to have the skills of our very talented designer, Chris Chisnall of OneCC Creative, and we would not have a book without our publisher, Robbie Burton of Craig Potton Publishing, who has guided us through every step in the process with a savvy wealth of experience.

Lucy Halsey

Project Co-ordinator/Editor

INTROD

Nestled in the centre of New Zealand on the edge of Tasman Bay, surrounded by hills and distant mountains, is a small city renowned for its natural environment, cultural life and superb weather. Nelson's generous attributes have always attracted a vibrant range of people and this is reflected in the diversity of culinary styles found here. Many Nelsonians enjoy growing food, hunting, foraging and fishing and then preparing and sharing it with others, while fresh local produce is easy to find in the excellent local markets, specialty shops, restaurants, cafés and food carts in the streets of central Nelson.

In the heart of Nelson is Nelson Central School within walking distance of the CBD, the museum, Suter Art Gallery, the Maitai River and the Centre of New Zealand. Nelson Central has an active School Community Group, and the idea for *Food Central* arose as an alternative to the usual fundraising gala, but also from a desire to contribute something more lasting to our community. What was conceived as a simple cookbook has grown into something much larger, carried by the enthusiasm of the wider community to share their food stories and recipes.

Needless to say, a cookbook is not a new way to raise funds. In 1948 the Nelson Central Home and School Association produced a cookbook complete with a handful of coloured photos, a foreword from Nelson's School Medical Officer and local advertising. We are happy to be following in this tradition, and hope that *Food Central* will endure as a significant celebration of the rich and diverse food culture of Nelson City.

Using the book

Lengthy instructions can take away the fun of experimentation and the element of surprise that make cooking special. However, in trying the recipes, we have found that some measuring is vital. We used conversion charts in books and on the internet and the children discovered that not all tablespoons were created equal. Suffice to say that despite our best efforts to standardise measurements, many recipes were left as they were for authenticity. The best advice we can offer, to avoid brain-strain and frustration with baking, is to invest in a set of measuring spoons and good digital kitchen scales.

We hope that you will use recipes as they are but also as inspiration for your own twist on things. With this in mind, the sections are by no means fixed. One person's snack is another's main. A soup or pie may be a main, as may a salad and bread. The sweet treats can be eaten for dessert or afternoon tea, with some making a delicious breakfast.

UCTION

Our Motto
"Aim High"
NELSON CENTRAL
HOME AND SCHOOL
ASSOCIATION
COOKERY
BOOK
2/6
FRUIT SALAD IN JELLY
GELATINE
ICE CREAM PUDDING.
MARSHMALLOW PUDDING.

'They love hearing about the two teachers that were here when I was a child, who are still here today. Nelson Central School is so special that some people just don't want to leave!'

Erina Tuhakaraina

Snacks & Sides

Gluten-free Cheese Crackers

These crackers remind me of winter afternoons in North Canterbury, when Mum had been baking and I would walk into a kitchen full of wonderful baking smells. After a long ride in the school bus and a busy day at school it was magic. Of course Mum never baked gluten-free, so I have converted these to gluten-free. All of the gluten-free ingredients are available from Bin Inn*. To convert back to the original recipe, simply replace all the flours and guar gum with 1 cup plain flour.

¾ cup white rice flour*
¼ cup arrowroot (tapioca) flour*
¼ cup potato flour*
pinch salt
pinch cayenne pepper
½ tsp guar gum*
30g butter (softened)
100g tasty cheese, grated
sesame seeds, to sprinkle (optional)
1 Tbsp ground linseed (optional)

Put all dry ingredients in food processor and mix to combine (or mix by hand).

Add butter, mix well and add cheese, mixing again.

While mixer is running, slowly add cold water (approx ⅓ cup) until you have a stiff dough. Check often as it's hard to tell what dough is like without feeling it.

The water amount will depend on how fine the flours are milled. If you add too much by mistake simply mix in some more flour.

Roll out on a floured surface until thin (doesn't matter how thin but thinner will create a crisper cracker). Cut into desired shapes. I sometimes do round ones with a cutter or simply cut into thin long rectangles with a knife.

Bake at 190°C until nice and golden.

Before cutting rolled out dough I often wet dough lightly and sprinkle with sesame seeds. You can also add ground linseed (one heaped tablespoon) to add fibre but you will need to add more water.

I often make a double recipe as they do not last long!

Wendy O'Connor

HAVEN
FISH & CHIPS
HAVEN ROAD FISH & CHIPS
OPEN
OPEN

Chilli Sweet Potato and Eggplant Crisps

1 orange sweet potato (300g) (any kumara is nice)

1 slender eggplant (350g)

¼ tsp ground coriander

1 tsp chicken salt

¼ tsp ground chilli powder

oil for deep frying

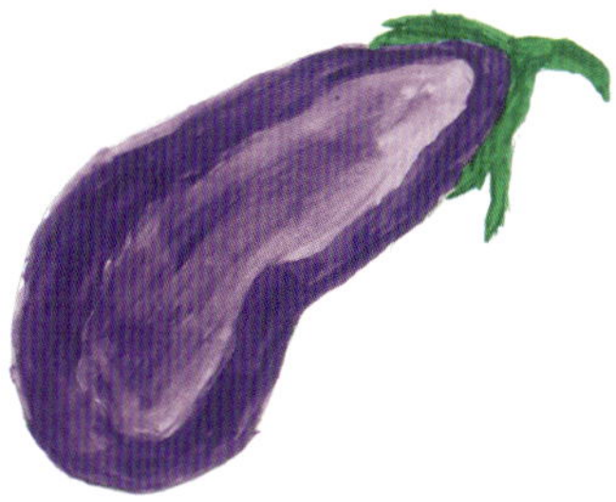

Peel sweet potato. Cut sweet potato and eggplant into long thin strips, similar in size. Place in a large bowl and mix.

Heat oil in a deep, heavy-based pan. Gently lower half the combined sweet potato and eggplant into the moderately hot oil. Cook over medium-high heat for 10 minutes or until golden and crisp. Carefully remove the crisps from the oil with tongs or slotted spoon. Drain on paper towels. Repeat cooking process with remaining sweet potato and egg-plant.

Combine chilli, coriander and salt in a small bowl. Sprinkle all the mixture over hot crisps. Toss until well coated. Serve immediately.

Kathryn Robertson

Grilled Tomatoes with Bruschetta

1 loaf Italian bread

4 large ripe tomatoes

4 Tbsp olive oil

2 Tbsp red wine vinegar

1 tsp soft brown sugar

salt and freshly ground pepper, to taste

½ tsp fresh chopped or dried marjoram leaves (or fresh basil)

1 clove garlic, cut in half

½ cup chopped, marinated artichokes, undrained

1 Tbsp finely chopped flat-leaf parsley

Cut bread into thick slices. Preheat grill.

Cut tomatoes in half; gently squeeze out seeds. Place tomatoes cut-side up in shallow, ovenproof dish.

Place herbs, salt and pepper, 2 Tbsp of oil, vinegar and sugar in a small screw-top jar and shake well. Pour dressing over tomatoes.

Cook tomatoes under hot grill for 30 minutes; turn after 15 minutes. Remove from heat and keep warm.

Brush bread liberally with rest of oil on both sides; toast until golden. Rub cut surface of garlic over bread. Place cooked tomatoes onto bread, top with artichokes and sprinkle with parsley.

Serve immediately.

Kathryn Robertson

Kendall's Hummus

1 tin chickpeas, 390g
(keep brine for thinning)

2-3 cloves chopped garlic

pinch of salt

juice of 1 large lemon

3 Tbsp tahini

3 Tbsp olive oil

2 Tbsp sweet chilli sauce (optional)

Put all ingredients in a blender and blend to a paste.

To flavour add 2 Tbsp of sweet chilli sauce and mix well.

Kendall Borland

Cobb Loaf with Spinach Dip

I used to make this quite often for our mothers' group when my son was young. It isn't super healthy, but it sure is delicious, and be careful... it is very addictive! You can make this up the night before and refrigerate and if you add lemon juice to the dip the vitamin C may help with the absorption of the iron in the spinach.

1 cobb loaf

2 small (250g) containers sour cream

1 packet French onion soup

1 packet frozen spinach (350g)

1 small tin water chestnuts

Defrost spinach and drain excess water. Mix all ingredients, except bread, with a stick blender and blend thoroughly. Cool mixture in the fridge. Slice top off a cobb loaf and remove most of the soft bread, leaving a good 'crust'. Place the loaf on a large platter, fill with the mixture and surround with pieces of the soft bread and top of loaf. Add a cut up French stick or other bread to ensure there is enough.

June Fallen

Potato Focaccia Bread

I get asked for this recipe a lot, so I may as well share it with the whole community!

Originally the idea is from an Annabel Langbein recipe but I've tinkered with it to make it more reliable in making a starter dough first. It's a very moist dough so don't be tempted to keep adding flour and try not to handle it too much. After the first rise, tip into a big baking dish lined with baking paper and sprinkle some flour over the dough to enable gentle spreading out, without getting into a great big sticky old mess.

This also makes a great pizza base or you can twist it into bread sticks, whatever takes your fancy!

250g potatoes peeled and chopped (2-3 medium to large sized potatoes)

1½ cups luke warm (not hot) water

1½ tsp yeast

¼ cup olive oil

2 tsp salt

4½ - 5 cups flour

Boil potatoes in salted water until tender. Drain, mash, and let cool for a bit.

Mix potatoes, water, yeast, and 1 cup of the flour together.

Let sit for a few minutes, can be up to 15-20 minutes depending on the temperature of the room, leave until bubbly and yeast is activated. (The combined temperature of the cooked potatoes and the warm water is really important. If you have it too warm the yeast won't activate and you'll have flat bread.)

Add remaining flour and other ingredients and mix. (This is good to do with a dough hook in a mixer if you have one, otherwise you can mix with a big wooden spoon.)

Cover and leave to rise in a warm place until doubled in size. Tip onto baking tray, cover and rise again.

When risen well, drizzle with extra olive oil and add olives, fresh herbs, especially oregano/thyme and a grind of salt before cooking.

Bake 200°C for 18 - 20 minutes.

Jane Murray

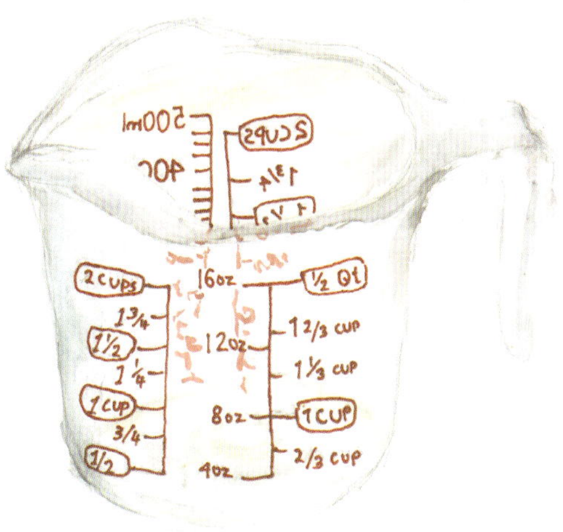

MAKO

MAERSK
MAERSK SEALAND
NO ENTRY
NO FISHING PAST THIS POINT

ROW

In 1992, having just returned from a chef's job in London and some travel around Europe, Nelson seemed quiet and I needed a project. It was the time to eat the food I most loved - outdoors. Some people bought a house with that Post Office home loan but I bought a restaurant and so from a 'Hole in the Wall' Broccoli Row began. People were cautious but we were eager to educate, and very quickly they returned for our tapas, focaccia bread, fresh seafood stews, lunch salads and cakes. They were ready for the best of the region's produce, simply prepared and all cooked on site. We had vegetables grown for us by Jimmy, we collected paddle crabs from the waterfront, we grew our own herbs, we worked long days and we loved it!

We grew to the point where suppliers had to change and the crabs arrived by taxi, but it was still very important that all food was local and produced on site, as it is to this day. A special project arrived, our son Tim, and nights were cut back. Then down came the building, but I couldn't let go and so I catered the food that Nelson people had all come to know. Two years on, along came a doctor who wanted a café at his medical centre. Would I do it again? Why wouldn't I? With a continual team of fantastic chefs, our food has evolved over the last 20 years but certain favourites have remained the same, one of those being Seafood Chowder. So here's how we make it. (Serves 6)

Sue McNulty

Seafood Chowder

1 onion, finely diced
1 red pepper, finely diced
1 stalk celery, finely diced
4 cloves fresh garlic, crushed
pinch of cayenne
1 dessert spoon tomato paste
200g butter
200g flour
fish stock
salt and pepper to taste
parsley, finely chopped
400g fresh seafood of choice, chopped

Sauté all vegetables in butter until cooked. Add cayenne and flour and cook out until this mix reaches a sandy texture. Add tomato paste and mix well.

Slowly add stock, mixing constantly to get a smooth texture. Amount of stock varies according to liquid in seafood and how thick you like your soup. Add seafood and seasoning. Bring to the boil to cook seafood completely and serve.

Tim makes (great) coffee for the food photo shoot.

Carrot and Coriander Soup

450g carrots
1 Tbsp vegetable oil
40g margarine
1 onion chopped
1 celery stalk chopped
1 litre vegetable stock
3 tsp ground coriander
1 Tbsp fresh coriander
salt and freshly ground black pepper

Chop the carrots – peel if necessary, heat the oil and 25g of the margarine in a large saucepan and fry the onion for a few minutes until soft but not browned. Add the chopped celery to the onion, cook briefly then add the carrots. Fry over a gentle heat for 3 - 4 minutes making sure that the vegetables do not stick to the pan. Add the stock, bring to the boil, and partially cover and simmer for about 10 minutes until the carrots are tender. Melt the rest of the margarine in a clean pan and fry the ground coriander for about 1 minute stirring constantly. Add the chopped fresh coriander. Process the soup in a food processor or blender, stir in the coriander mixture and season. Before serving you can add a little milk or lemon juice.

Jenny Hitchings

Chicken Tom Yum

Matika makes this whenever anyone in the family has a cold. It is so magic that our matriarch, who never used to eat spicy food, recommends it to everyone. You can leave out the chicken and use more mushrooms instead.

2 sticks lemon grass
galangal 3-4 slices (blue ginger)
4-6 kaffir lime leaves
1 Tbsp (or more) tamarind paste
1 onion or some shallots, cut in chunks
3-4 button mushrooms, cut in chunks
400g chicken (legs or wings with bones)
chilli (if you like it hot)
soy sauce (to taste)
fish sauce (to taste)
fresh coriander leaves, if available
cooked rice (optional, as a side dish)

Boil some water (4 cups) and add the lemon grass, galangal, kaffir leaves, tamarind, onion and chilli. Boil for about 2 minutes, until the tamarind dissolves.

Take bones out of chicken and add them to the liquid and boil for 5 minutes.

Cut the meat into small chunks and add with mushrooms to pot.

Season with soy and fish sauces and boil for a few minutes, until the chicken is cooked.

Serve 'holus bolus' with fresh chopped coriander and a side bowl of rice for each person.

The Adams-Halsey Clan

Minestrone

This soup gets better with age, and will last up to 5 days in a cold fridge.

50g butter

50g each of onion, carrots, leeks, celery and cabbage

50g flour

1.5 litres stock (vegetable)

2 Tbsp tomato puree

½ cup spaghetti (or shorter pasta such as risoni)

1 cup potato - diced

tomato, diced

bacon, diced

garlic, diced

parsley, chopped

¼ cup peas

parmesan croutons

In a heavy based pot, sauté carrots, celery, onion, leeks and potato in the butter. Add enough flour to this to soak up the butter, continue to sauté until flour turns 'blonde', then add the stock, followed by all other ingredients, except parsley and peas.

Bring to the boil then immediately turn down the heat to a low simmer.

Simmer until the pasta and potatoes are well cooked.

Add peas just before serving.

Serve with parmesan croutons and parsley.

Angela Kernohan, Melrose House Café

Wednesday night riders set off from Central School

Noodle Soup

My memories are often food orientated. Mum and Dad were always trying out the latest 70's fad, such as yoghurt bugs, homemade salamis, ginger beer and cherry wine for the grown ups. We grew up in Hanmer Springs and I have lovely memories of hunting for mushrooms on the Molesworth road and fossicking for chestnuts in the hospital grounds with whanau and friends. I also remember Dad mastering the art of what he called 'Arab bread'. This was a flatbread similar to the one I get to make my pita chips. We would take Arab bread and salad with us when we went swimming up the river. Dad would make a fire and cook saussies and we would use the bread as a plate and then eat it once we were done.

This soup recipe reminds me of how much food has changed in my lifetime. I feed our tribe noodle soup regularly. It appeals because the base uses a chicken carcass left over from the Sunday roast. It has the fusion of the hearty taste that you get from Mama's soup and a light Asian food experience. You can throw in any kind of noodles you like including '2 minute' ones if your kids haven't quite got a grasp on 'udon' yet! Makes 4 portions.

1 roast chicken carcass

chicken stock: drain off any juice from roast, remove fat when cool and add to broth

1 onion

4 cloves of garlic

1 dessert spoon, grated fresh ginger

chilli, as much as you like, finely chopped

small dash of sesame oil, as it is quite potent

a good slosh of peanut oil

miso paste to taste

vegetables of choice eg. carrots, peas, corn, beans, broccoli, bamboo shoots

noodles, 1 serving per person (I use udon)

juice of 1 lemon or lime

fresh herbs

Sweat onion in oils until clear. Add chicken carcass, garlic, ginger and chilli. Sauté for about 1 minute to release the flavours. Add water and any stock from chicken and bring to the boil. Simmer for 30 minutes. Remove chicken carcass and take off any meat. This meat can go back into the pot. Add vegetables (hardest ones first) and miso paste to taste. When cooked through, add noodles. If you don't feel like there is enough meat you can add slices of grilled pork strips on top. Cashew nuts or tofu work well too.

Squeeze some lemon or lime juice on top and add any herbs you have in the garden or supermarket. I use a mixture of spring onions, Vietnamese mint, coriander, basil and calendula petals depending on what is available. Serve with extra chilli for those who like it hot.

Sally Craighead

RUGBY
I'M WITH THE
BAND-IT

'Many older Nelsonians will remember the warm sweet smells from the Griffin and Son's factory wafting over the city. It is such a strong memory for me that I can still smell it. The daily five o'clock punctuation of the Griffin's steam whistle, signalling the end of another shift, was woven into our lives.'

Pete Rainey

Granddad Day's Best Fish Picnic

Granddad Day has lived in Nelson all his life and has been fishing from Okiwi Bay (in Croiselles Harbour, up the coast from Nelson) for 62 years. This is his favourite recipe - for life as well as for the meal!

fishing boat and accessories, including a gas cooker
small frying pan
butter
fresh white bread
picnic utensils

Launch the boat and go fishing.

Catch quota of Blue Cod or similar.

Find a nice quiet beach with a good landing spot and unload boat.

Gut and fillet some of the fish.

Set up gas cooker and frying pan.

Gently fry fillets in a little butter.

Wrap fish in white bread smeared with butter.

Eat!!

Jacqui Day, Jemma and Sam Mead

Bill's Fabulous Flash-Fried Paua

This recipe starts at the beach after you have gathered the paua. The most important part of this recipe is how you treat the paua immediately after you have gathered them. Warning: do not read on if you are at all squeamish as this requires a bit of brutality towards the paua. Immediately after shucking the paua, you need to bash the paua meat. Some people use a hammer but we use a piece of wood. You need to deliver two hard blows to the meat followed by several lesser blows around the outside edge. This ensures that the paua meat is tenderised and not rubbery and chewy. Securing the shucked paua in a cloth or onion bag is a good idea to stop it slipping around as you bash it.

Back at home, you will need:
2 paua (legal size) prepared as above
2 cloves of garlic
2 spring onions
2cm piece of peeled fresh ginger
juice of one lemon
1 Tbsp (or 15ml) of soy sauce
Oil (peanut is best)
Salt and ground black pepper

Rinse paua in cold water to remove any grit. Slice very thinly with a sharp knife. Set aside. Finely chop garlic, ginger and spring onion and divide in half. Heat a skillet (or other heavy based fry pan) until smoking, with sufficient oil to coat the bottom. Add salt and pepper and half the paua together with half the garlic, ginger and spring onions. Stir fry at high heat for about one minute. Add half the lemon juice and half the soy sauce. Briefly stir then remove from the pan. Quickly clean the pan, add more oil to coat and wait until it is smoking before repeating this procedure with the second lot of paua and other ingredients. This is the second most important part of the recipe, the pan has to be really hot and the paua cooked in small batches in order that it cooks very quickly and stays tender. Paua prepared and cooked in this way will be light and delicate and not at all chewy!!

Gill Rowe

Ray Day catches hapuku for lunch in Tasman Bay

Mussel Fritters

If using fresh mussels, fifteen to twenty mussels should yield 250-300g of meat.

The mussels should be scrubbed well under cold running water (discard any that don't close), then steam open in a little water in a pan with a tight fitting lid. Give the mussels plenty of heat and remove the pan as they open.

250g mussel meat
2 eggs separated
¼ cup each: flour, milk
1 large handful parsley
1 large spring onion
vegetable oil

Mince the mussel meat in a food processor with the spring onion and parsley.

Combine egg yolks, flour and milk to make a batter. Mix in the minced mussel mix.

Season with salt and pepper. Set aside. Whisk egg whites until stiff and fold into mussel mix.

Heat enough oil in a frying pan to shallow fry the fritters.
Use a dessertspoon to measure dollops into the hot oil. Cook on both sides over medium heat until fritters are crispy brown and cooked through.

Serve with lemon juice mixed with mayonnaise as a dip.
(See mayonnaise recipe p. 61)

Alex Chisnall

Daddy's Secret Raw Fish Recipe

This is my happy soul food as it reminds me of my dad. He used to make it on Christmas Day and would never give me the recipe, so I had to watch him make it. Which I did. This is the first time I've put it to paper.

1-2 fillets of white fish (moki, snapper, terakihi)
lemon juice
1-2 cans of coconut cream
red capsicum, spring onions, red onions, tomatoes (optional)

Cut up fish into cubes and place in a deep bowl

Cover fish with lemon juice and leave for a few hours or overnight, the fish is ready when it turns white.

Drain off excess juice, add any of the optional ingredients
(I like raw fish simple)

Salt to taste

Add coconut cream

Ta daa! You're done.

DD

Chicken Nuggets

All kids love these and they are so quick and easy that kids can make them. Please don't feel that you have to follow the recipe exactly, every batch varies and still gets eaten. Using rice bubbles instead of breadcrumbs means they are great for kids with a gluten intolerance and also provides a tasty, crispy coating. Makes about 25.

300g chicken mince
2 free range eggs
1½ cups rice bubbles
2 Tbsp cooking oil
salt to taste

Lightly whisk eggs in a bowl.

Add the rest of the ingredients and mix well.

Using a fork, splodge out nuggets of the mixture into a hot frying pan.

Turn over when underside is brown.

Rebecca Fyfe

Cheesy Sausages in Bacon

A twist on 'devils-on-horseback' with sausages instead of prunes, this recipe is from one of my well-loved German cookbooks. You can make it with any type of sausage but I think Bockwurst is best and if you are keen to try it, my friend Doris Faulhaber has all kinds of sausage and bacon to choose from at her Saturday or Wednesday market stalls in Nelson. It is best to preheat the sausages before putting them on the barbecue or in the pan, especially if the bacon is a quick frying one. Serves 4.

4 sausages, bockwurst, fleischwurst, knobliener or nuernberger-stadtwurst
1 Tbsp oil
1 level tsp paprika powder
150g block of cheese: gouda or edam
2 Tbsp mild mustard
2 Tbsp ketchup
8 thin slices of bacon

Slit the sausages lengthwise and brush thinly with a mixture of oil and paprika.

Cut the cheese into four, long, even strips and squeeze the cheese into the slit in each sausage. Mix the mustard with the ketchup and brush the sausage with this mixture. Wrap two slices of bacon around each sausage, fastening with toothpicks if necessary.

Heat up the barbecue or frying pan and cook sausages, turning frequently until the bacon is evenly cooked and the cheese melted.

Great served with beer, tomato salad and a hunk of baguette.

Gabi Borowsky

Nelson Cathedral - looking towards Sir Stanley Whitehead Walkway on eastern hills

"CENTRE OF NEW ZEALAND"
THIS SIGNAL PRESENTED TO THE CITY
TO MARK THE 21ST ANNIVERSARY OF
NELSON JAYCEE, AUGUST 1968.
TRIG. B.H. IS THE POINT OF ORIGIN
FOR SURVEYS IN THE NELSON DISTRI

KA★PIE

When we were kids Mum had us cooking dinner for the family once a week. Once we'd mastered a few basic skills the choice of what we were having for dinner was up to us. More often than not, my choice was to cook the family a bacon and egg pie. Not because it's so delicious, though it is. Not because it's so easy, though it is. Not because it's so economical, though it is. Not because the leftovers were perfect for our school lunchboxes the next day, though they were.

For me, it was all about the decorations I could make with the spare pastry on top of the pie. The thing is you eat with your eyes before you taste with your mouth, and food that looks great is just tastier. Sometimes I'd sculpt out a forest scene with vines, berries, birds and other wild creatures. Other weeks every piece of pie would have individual names drawn in ornate script for each member of the family.

My love for bacon and egg pies has only grown, until six years ago, when I couldn't stop myself buying the corner pie shop on Nile Street and opening Ka-Pie. Now every time I'm feeling nostalgic, my darling husband brings me a delicious bacon and egg pie hot from the oven.

Lou Hayes

Easy-As Bacon and Egg Pie

This is enough to serve four, with maybe some left over for lunch boxes the next day. Try using other meats too. Shaved smoked ham is a cheaper alternative to bacon and imparts a lovely flavour to the pie; we also use sausage. Or go vege and add herbs and spinach, tomato and sautéed onion, anything goes! Buy ready-made pastry for super convenience, or try out this fabulous rich and flaky recipe, that you can make entirely in a food processor or by hand.

Quick Pastry

2½ cups flour

2 tsp baking powder

pinch of salt

250g cold butter

about 1 cup milk, water or combination of both

1 tsp wine or cider vinegar (optional)

Pie

pastry

12 or so eggs

1 rasher bacon per person

cheese

salt and pepper

Mix flour, baking powder and salt. Add butter (in cubes) and cut into flour. Don't overdo this step, you still want to see a few chunks of butter when you roll it out. Acidify your liquid with the vinegar if you want super tender pastry, then add to the flour mixture in a thin stream while pulsing your blender (or cut into mixture using a knife) until it forms a ball of dough. Roll out thinly on a floured bench.

Pre-heat oven to 200°C

Grease a pie dish. You can use any ovenproof dish. I use roasting pans or cake pans as the metal helps with making a crispy bottom.

Line the dish with pastry and sprinkle some grated cheese over. Break in eggs. Cut bacon into pie using scissors. Season generously with salt and pepper. Prick yolks and gently swirl eggs to create a marbled effect. Sprinkle some more cheese and top with pastry, gluing down edges with some of the egg mixture.

Go to town decorating the top with the leftover pastry. Flowers, vines, berries, lettering, trucks and tanks! Brush a little milk over pastry for a glaze.

Bake for about 45 minutes. Pastry needs a hot oven to kick start, but you can turn your oven down after 20 minutes or so if it looks like the pastry will brown before the filling will cook (largely depends on which dish you are using) you can also loosely cover dish with baking paper to slow down browning.

Easy as. Ka Pie!

For variety Naomi Stephenson adds 3 large sliced tomatoes and a tin of drained peas to her bacon and egg pie and the cheese is optional.

Spinach and Feta Pie

I started making this pie about six years ago and since then have made it once a week for dinner, to give to friends and to take to pot-lucks. It is very easy to make, healthy and everyone likes it - even children. My Dad calls it the 'Green Party Pie'.

Base

1 cup oats

1 cup flour (plain, wholemeal or wheat free)

½ cup oil (I prefer olive oil)

½ cup water

Filling

spinach, one packet frozen (350g) or a large bunch freshly steamed

feta, ¾ packet

8 eggs

Topping

seeds – mixture sesame, pumpkin, sunflower

grated cheese

Make the base a bit ahead of time if you are organised and think of it. Put oats and flour in a bowl and mix. Make a well and pour in the water and oil and mix it up. Not essential, but if you have time, place in the fridge for at least 1 hour. Heat oven to 200°C. Press base mixture into a pie dish with sides (I use a flan dish). Cook it for about ten minutes whilst you are preparing the filling. Crack the eggs into a bowl and beat well. Add the spinach, crumbled up feta and a little cracked pepper. Pour the filling on the slightly cooked base. Sprinkle a topping of the seeds and some grated cheese – just the amount that you like. Cook for about 30 minutes. It is cooked when the mixture is firm and the base crust is golden. Either eat straight away or let it cool and eat warm a bit later.

We serve it with tomato relish and homemade mayonnaise (see mayonnaise recipe p. 61)

Georgie Pattullo

Mini Pumpkin Quiches

A delicious snack or light lunch. These can be made as a vegetarian version too, with corn instead of bacon. Yummy hot or cold, they make an excellent addition to lunch boxes. Makes 24 small quiches.

3 sheets short pastry

3 bacon rashers (finely chopped)- plus a bit extra for the top

1 onion (finely chopped)

⅔ cup mashed pumpkin

1 cup grated cheese

1 egg lightly beaten

¼ cup milk

pinch nutmeg

Cut pastry into 7cm circles with a fluted cutter and press into shallow patty tins. Cook bacon and onion in fry pan until crisp and drain. Stir bacon mixture into combined pumpkin, cheese, egg, milk and nutmeg. Spoon into pastry cases.

Cut extra bacon into thin strips, roll up and place a piece on each quiche. Bake at 200°C for 15 minutes. Reduce heat to 180°C and bake 10 mins or until golden brown.

June Fallen

Lambretta's

Just as the Lambretta scooter from Italy was designed to be an accessible and affordable form of transport for all, Lambretta's Café, on the sunny side of Hardy Street, was established for everyone to feel welcome.

Originally opened with four business partners, Rob McKegney (the well known Restauranteur of The Hitching Post in the 1980s), chef Steve Russell and well-travelled Nelson couple, Rhys Odey and Leanne Murray. Rhys and Leanne, whose two sons attend Nelson Central School, have been the sole owners since 2005.

The prominent large pillars out the front of the building are from the same era as the Lambretta. Inside 1950s nostalgia meets a comfortable and familiar atmosphere.

There are five scooters around the café and many an interesting story has been told by customers who've owned a Lambretta themselves. There is also a sticker wall where people can send in photos of Lambretta's café stickers in different places all over the world.

Our pizzas are named after Lambretta models and parts, like the 'loose wheel' and 'SX200'.

Rob's early influence helped us create a great gourmet pizza menu, the sauce we still use today has its origins in those famous Hitching Post pizzas. Team your pizza with some fresh, locally grown salad greens and garlic aioli or sweet chilli jam.

Leanne Murray

Provençal Sauce (Tomato-based sauce for pizza)

4 x 400g tins of tomatoes (whole or crushed) or 1kg fresh

¼ cup of olive oil

2 tsp salt

2 tsp black pepper

2 tsp crushed garlic

handful of fresh basil or Tbsp of dried

Put all ingredients together and blend with stick blender or whiz until spreadable.

Lambretta's
CAFE - BAR
NAL BEER
Lambretta's
STELLA ARTOIS
STELLA ARTOIS
22

Chilli Jam

A perfect preserve to donate to Mrs Harrison's Bottles at the school gala, if you have any left to spare.

4 x 400g tins of tomatoes (whole or crushed) or 1 kg fresh tomatoes
250g white sugar
2 tsp crushed fresh ginger
4 tsp crushed fresh garlic
4 tsp tomato paste
2 level tsp salt
½ tsp chilli flakes
½ tsp chilli powder

Put all ingredients in a big pot and blend with a stick blender or do in kitchen whiz. Once all blended then heat, stirring constantly. Bring to boil and simmer for 20 – 30 minutes. Bottle up in sterilized bottles or jars. We cook it until it is a pouring consistency.

Leanne Murray (Lambretta's)

Garlic Aioli

A delicious addition to most meals, especially for drizzling and dipping.

3 eggs
2 Tbsp white vinegar
1 dessert spoon whole grain mustard
½ tsp salt
½ tsp black pepper
1 tsp crushed garlic
2 cups of canola oil (or any taste free oil)

Put all ingredients, except the oil, in food processor. Blend until mixture combines and starts to lighten, then slowly drizzle in the 2 cups of oil while blending at a constant speed - mixture may split if this is done too quickly. As a variation you can add lemon or fresh herbs for a different flavour.

Leanne Murray (Lambretta's)

Stirling Sports
andbags
travelsmart

Bakery
Cobbler

THE BOAT SHED

Broad Bean Crusader Salad

This is a favourite salad at our house in early summer when our huge broad bean patch has weathered the spring winds and finally yielded the first fresh beans. We either eat this as a salad or spoon it onto good bread – toasted sourdough is delicious. Add more olive oil and salt of course, and you have a great lunch.

2 cups, (shelled) fresh new season's broad beans

Neudorf's Mt Crusader fresh sheep milk cheese (it has an unripened soft lemony taste)

lemon zest

good olive oil

salt and pepper

We don't bother to peel the broad beans as their coats are still tender and delicious. Gather the pods and pop the beans out of their furry sleeping bags. Boil them for 1 minute in salted water, then drain and plunge into cold water to keep their beautiful colour. Put the drained beans into a bowl and throw through the olive oil, lemon zest, salt and a good grind of fresh black pepper. Sometimes I throw in a few of the broad bean shoots for crunch and texture, or a scattering of marigold petals. Tear up about half of the cheese into bite sized pieces and throw this through the beans and dressing. You can buy the Mt Crusader cheese at the Nelson Market in summer at the Neudorf Dairy stall, or from local supermarkets.

Josephine Cachemaille

Barbecued Marinated Vegetables

3 slender eggplants

3 medium zucchini

1 medium red onion

1 medium red capsicum

2 cloves garlic, crushed

2 tsp chopped fresh thyme leaves

1 medium green capsicum

2 tsp finely chopped fresh basil

¼ cup olive oil

2 Tbsp balsamic vinegar

Cut eggplant and zucchini into diagonal 2 cm-thick slices.

Cut capsicum into 2 cm-wide strips, and onion into eight wedges.

Place all vegetables into a large mixing bowl. Add the garlic, herbs, olive oil and vinegar, toss lightly to combine. Cover with plastic wrap and let stand for 1 hour.

Preheat barbecue. Drain vegetables from marinade. Place on lightly greased grill or hotplate. Cook over medium-high heat for 8-10 minutes, until tender and slightly charred.

Serve with barbecued meat.

Kathryn Robertson

Simply Scrumptious Salad

This is not a recipe but a way to make a salad that is never dull. I was taught how to make a green salad by my Granny Rhoda, who learned the art of simple cooking when she lived in the French Alps as a newly-wed. We all have favourite variations on this theme in my family, but the secret is making fresh dressing for each salad in the bottom of the bowl. The key components are oil and an acid, plus or minus a sweet element. I was brought up to just use olive oil, lemon juice and Dijon mustard (Granny used a pinch of sugar too). This is our nightly ritual, year round, with whatever raw salad ingredients we have on hand. I have no problem getting help from our children as it is considered a nice job. In winter I use the same principle for a crunchy cabbage slaw. My mother would also pop in chopped orange and apple to add interest and vitamins to the slaw.

Get a salad bowl - a decent wooden one is best.

Wash lettuce leaves, shake and leave to drain.

Pour in good quality olive oil (about a tablespoon) or macadamia or avocado oil.

Splash in either lemon juice or vinegar of your choice to taste (our kids love balsamic).

You can then add a small teaspoon of whole seed mustard and, if you like garlic, rub a cut clove around the bowl with some dressing. A grind of black pepper and salt are optional.

Give it a quick stir and throw in the salad ingredients.

I tend to put avocado in first so that it sits in the dressing and is hidden from any greedy vultures. The ingredients are flexible, from just lettuce, with or without other salad leaves, cucumber, tomatoes and capsicum, to whole Kalamata olives, cherry tomatoes and feta cheese for a Greek salad. Nasturtium flowers add prettiness and a peppery bite. Just don't go mad with cutting things up too small or a crisp salad turns to a mushy coleslaw.

Toss just before eating.

Best eaten at the end of the main meal to refresh the palate.

Lucy Halsey

Raisin and Coriander Rice

Here's a recipe that I like, however my kids won't go near it! A colourful accompaniment that goes well with meat, chicken or fish. It combines well with a beef stroganoff to give a lighter flavour. If coriander isn't in season, I use any other chopped fresh herbs.

2 Tbsp vegetable oil
6-8 spring onions
1 red capsicum, finely chopped
¼ cup raisins
2½ cups cooked long grain rice
finely grated zest of 2 limes or 1 lemon
salt and pepper to taste
3 Tbsp finely chopped coriander

Heat the oil in a large frypan. Add the spring onion and cook for a few minutes until slightly softened. Add the capsicum, raisins, rice and lime zest. Cook for 8-10 minutes until heated through. Season to taste then toss in the chopped coriander.

From: *Rice, Pasta and Potatoes* by Deb Crosby. *New Zealand Good Food* series.

Angela Craig

THE BOAT SHED CÁFE

I can remember saying to one of my parents some years ago 'there is absolutely no *#^%g way in the world I would own a restaurant in Nelson... except...maybe, the Boat Shed?' Time certainly has moved on. Firstly I don't swear any more, chefs rarely do, and I find myself standing at the stove in the restaurant with its feet in the water and loving it!

The waterfront is a beautiful place to live and work. The sun setting over Haulashore, spring tides, the crashing of waves against the sea wall, the fishing - you can catch snapper right out in front of the Boat Shed. I have lent rods to friends to catch kahawai around the café's legs. But, and most might find this peculiar, what I really love about the area is the working aspect of our port. The fishing boats, container or timber ships, it's all fascinating. I don't even mind being serenaded to sleep by the crash and bang of containers being unloaded. It is all part of the charm.

A visitor to New Zealand once asked me,'What does that ship carry?' He was pointing to one of the enormous and slightly ridiculous looking floating blocks with a picture of a dolphin on the side of it. 'Oh that one, yes, full of dolphins. We like to eat on them on toast here.' He was appalled! Anyway, I set him straight, and then I served him his lunch - something on toast probably.

The Boat Shed food is simple, and designed to share. Here's a recipe, no dolphin, but cockles from Westhaven. There is nothing more basic and delicious than a bowl of shellfish thrown in the middle of the table family style, to fight over, with some good bread to mop up the juices.

Daniel Monopoli

Westhaven cockles with garlic, white wine and parsley butter

- 1.5kg fresh cockles
- 1 cup white wine
- 6 cloves garlic, chopped and peeled
- handful of the inner celery leaves, chopped
- 75g butter
- couple of large pinches of fresh parsley, roughly chopped

If the cockles are straight from the sea, place in a bucket of salt water for a few hours to purge them. Wash them well and place in a large pan with the wine, garlic and celery leaves. Put over a medium heat and let them steam open as the wine comes to the boil. As soon as all the cockles open, remove from the heat and discard any that refuse to open.

Tip out most of the liquid, leaving about 4 tablespoons in the pan with the cockles. Add the butter and parsley, and more garlic if you love it - then reheat the pan, shaking constantly. When hot, serve immediately, spooning the buttery juices over the cockles. Accompany with sourdough bread.

Serves 4.

Wine match: A Nelson Sauvignon Blanc.

Nam's Mushy Peas

What this classic northern English fare lacks aesthetically is returned abundantly in flavour! They taste wonderful with anything potato (fishcakes or lumberjack/oven fries or mashed potato) and with meat pies (hence the heralded 'pea, pie n pud'). Serves 4-6.

- 2 cup dried blue peas
- cold water
- 1 tsp each of sugar and salt
- vinegar for serving (typically malt vinegar)

Rinse peas then place in a large pan and fill until water level is about 2 inches above the peas. Soak overnight (peas will absorb water and swell).

The next day, thoroughly rinse peas in fresh running water and return to large pan.

Cover with sufficient water to just cover peas. Add sugar and salt and bring to boil.

Reduce heat and gently simmer, stirring occasionally, until peas soften and a thick 'gravy' develops (about 1 to 1½ hours). Add a little more water if peas are drying and lacking the 'gravy' element. Serve in generous portions with vinegar to taste.

See my recipe for Fishcakes to go with this. (p. 117).

Deb Hardcastle

Mayonnaise

All my extended family make this mayonnaise and have a jar in their fridges. I have made it for years. My husband, kids and any visitors love it. We eat it with salad, crispy potatoes, my spinach pie ... with almost anything.

- chopped garlic (as desired)
- 2 eggs
- 1 tsp honey
- 1 tsp grainy mustard
- 1 tsp salt
- a few herbs
- 2 cups light olive oil
- ¼ cup cider vinegar

Into a blender put the garlic, eggs, honey, mustard, salt and herbs. Blend on high for a few minutes. Then add the oil really slowly 1 Tbsp at a time. The mixture should start going very thick – like mayonnaise. Then add the vinegar.

I use olive oil and cider vinegar but have used other types and they all work.

Keeps in a jar in the fridge for up to 2 weeks.

Variations

For a thicker mayonnaise just use 3 egg yolks (not the whites) and at the very end add a Tbsp of boiling water. This makes a very thick, creamy mayonnaise.

Georgie Pattullo

Real Slow Cooked Onion and Garlic Gravy

Mum and Dad import awesome stainless steel barbecues and Dad loves cooking big slabs of meat on them. He is good at it too! We love this special gravy. He always makes a big jug of it. I enjoy helping Dad peel the onions and crush the garlic. I have to remember not to rub my eyes – it makes them cry! Onion and garlic help to keep the winter germs away, so that's cool.

- 8 medium size onions
- 10 cloves of locally grown garlic
- 1 cup stock (beef or chicken)
- 1 tsp salt
- 1 tsp pepper
- 1 Tbsp balsamic vinegar
- 1 Tbsp Worcestershire sauce
- 2 Tbsp olive oil

Peel and halve the onions, combine with the garlic, salt pepper and olive oil. Place in ovenproof non stick pot or ovenproof dish.

Gently fry over low heat on top of the stove for approx 20 min. or until the onions start to brown. Add the 2 Tbsp balsamic vinegar and 2 Tbsp Worcestershire sauce, stir well and place inside an oven preheated to 140˚C.

Cover and cook 2-3 hours.

When cooking is completed, remove from oven and pulp with kitchen hand whiz. Add stock and place back on oven top and reduce to desired thickness.

Serve in your favourite gravy boat – hot.

Paige Sofield

Pickled Figs

2 cups white vinegar
2 cups brown sugar
2 tsp whole cloves
half a cinnamon stick
2 tsp allspice
1.5 kg figs

Combine first five ingredients in a pot and bring to the boil. Simmer 5 minutes.

Strain syrup and discard spices. Cut figs in half and add to syrup. Simmer very gently for 8 minutes. Don't stir the fruit so as not to destroy the shape.

Pack into sterile jars and cover with syrup.

Kristin Tilley-Brown

Feijoa Chutney

2 cups feijoa flesh, chopped
1 large onion, peeled and diced
1 cup sultanas
1 cup firmly packed brown sugar
2 cups cider vinegar
1 tsp salt
¾ tsp ground cloves
½ Tbsp curry powder

Place all ingredients in a large, heavy based saucepan. Bring to boil stirring until sugar is dissolved.

Turn down heat and simmer hard 30-45 minutes, stirring regularly until thick and syrupy.

Ladle into sterilised jars. Be sure they are well sealed. Store in cool dark place.

Kristin Tilley-Brown

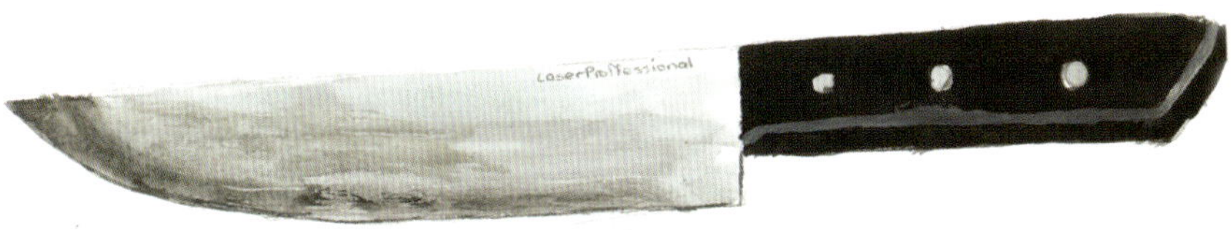

Mrs Harrison's Bottles

School galas are a highlight of every school calendar, with a great opportunity for the school and the wider community to get together. Nelson Central School is no exception. The front field, surrounded by historic lime trees, is a fabulous venue to set up marquees and makes a convivial setting for people to mingle. Each year there is an amazing array of food stalls. Devonshire teas, homemade sweets and cake stalls always sellout fast, as do waffles, nachos and sushi. Children suck on toffee apples and watch in amazement as spirals of fresh apple are produced by turning the handle on Jocelyn Smith's special apple device.

Then there are the other stalls, some of which almost count as food stalls. The garden stall always has great edibles and Dave Palmer's book stall, jammed with books, undoubtedly has recipe books and information on growing edible plants. Naturally, my favourite is "Mrs Harrison's Bottles" stall! The perfect stall to run as it requires very little preparation time, school-wide participation and no overheads. I simply ask each student to bring a bottle of their choice to school prior to the gala. Numbers are written underneath each bottle and the bottles are displayed to entice buyers. Numbered tickets are sold, with each ticket providing a chance to win the corresponding bottle, which of course is a mystery until the ticket is handed over.

The term "bottles" is loose, with a huge array of beautiful home made preserves through to shop bought toiletries, sauces, condiments, drinks and jars of sweets. More or less anything goes except alcohol, being a school event. The highlight for me is seeing the young boys arriving excitedly with their tickets, hoping for a big win, but leaving forlorn when having paused near the large bottle of cola, I move to give them the bottle of hot mustard sauce that bears the corresponding number to their ticket!

Christine Harrison
(Deputy Principal, Nelson Central School)

Tingy Lemonade

We have been making fizzy lemonade in Room 2. Our teacher Dave Palmer sends us to the staffroom in groups, to make it as part of our reading contracts. The recipe is from Jill Brasell in a School Journal from 1990 and it is really easy and fun to make. It tastes quite 'grown up' and is much nicer than bought lemonade. The yeast is what makes it fizzy.

2 litre clean plastic bottle with screw-on lid
3 lemons
1 cup sugar
¼ tsp granulated yeast
a jug for pouring

Pour the sugar into the jug and add enough hot water to dissolve the sugar and stir.

Cut lemons in half and squeeze the juice into the jug.

Pour the lemony mixture into the bottle and add cold water until it is about 5 cm from the top of the bottle. Add the yeast, screw on the lid and tip the bottle to mix.

Leave for about four days in place that isn't too hot or cold. Keep squeezing the bottle because when it feels hard to press it is ready. Refrigerate before drinking.

(Based on instructions from 'How to make fizzy lemonade' by Jill Brasell. School Journal Part 2, Number 4, 1990. Ministry of Education, Wellington)

THE MAIN EVENT

HEAVEN AND EARTH

The name of this recipe is so lovely and enticing. It is a favourite in our family and so easy to make. The girls love the sweet apple taste mixed with the yummy bacon. A real winter warmer.

1 kg potatoes, scrubbed and chunked

1 kg crisp apples, cored and chunked

2 or 3 thick slices streaky bacon, diced

butter or oil

salt

a few sprigs of marjoram, roughly chopped.

Put the potatoes to boil in plenty of salted water. After 10 minutes, add the apples and finish cooking both together, then drain.

Meanwhile fry the diced bacon in its own fat with as much butter or oil as you need to keep it from sticking. Remove the bacon and reheat the drippings in the pan and fry the potatoes and apples till they take a little colour. (You may need more oil or butter). Finish with the marjoram and then pile bacon, potatoes and apples into a hot dish to serve.

Harriet Denham

AUBERGINE AND COTTAGE CHEESE BAKE

I became a vegetarian over 40 years ago and things were very different then. It was the time of bean sprouts, homemade bread which weighed a ton, yoghurt in the hot water cupboard and beer brewing in the garage. We wore cheesecloth and Indian bling and were very earnest about various causes. Probably our more conventional neighbours saw us as a little mad.

Now it is quite respectable to be a vegetarian and there are many cookbooks and useful products which make it easy to produce interesting and nutritious meals.

1 largish aubergine

1 pottle of cottage cheese (200g)

juice and zest of 1 – 2 lemons

1 onion

3 cloves garlic

4 tomatoes

1 red or green pepper

fresh herbs – e.g. basil and parsley

seasoning to taste

Poach sliced aubergine for a few minutes until tender, drain well. Saute onion and garlic in a little oil, then stir into cottage cheese, adding lemon juice and zest. Chop tomatoes and pepper, season, adding chopped herbs. In a baking dish layer aubergine slices with the cottage cheese mixture and top with tomato mixture. Bake at 200°C for about 20 minutes.

Jenny Hitchings

CHINESE BARBECUE PORK

My mum used to always make this for special occasions when I was little. When I asked her for the recipe some years ago she gave me 'teaspoonish' quantities, with the words 'if you want it saltier add more salt, if you want it sweeter add more sugar!'

Working out the quantities for the sauce has been a bit tricky as I usually change the amount depending on the size of the piece of pork and what I have in the pantry. All quantities should be adjusted to taste.

shoulder or leg of pork

6 cloves garlic, crushed

2 tsp salt

2 tsp sugar

8 Tbsp light soy sauce

2 Tbsp golden syrup

1 tsp Chinese five spice

3 Tbsp black bean paste (I use Lee Kum Kee brand, from the international section of the supermarket)

Or

3 Tbsp Char Siu sauce (Lee Kum Kee brand)

2 Tbsp black bean paste

Trim off the excess fat and skin if you don't like your meat fatty, then prick all over.

Place in an oven proof dish or oven bag.

Mix garlic, salt, sugar, soy sauce and the choice of the other ingredients and marinate the pork for at least an hour.

Roast in oven at 180°C for 45 mins – 1 hour or until juices run clear for smaller pieces.

Serve with plain jasmine rice, stir-fried vegetables and jasmine tea.

Leftovers are great chopped up in noodle dishes.

Choi Fu

VEGETABLE AND LENTIL CURRY

This curry is delicious served with rice and naan bread. I like a dollop of sour cream and a splash of mango chutney on mine. Sweet Thai chilli sauce is also good on top. I have not put in any quantities as it is nice to have it slightly different each time.

onion (chopped)

garlic (grated or crushed)

celery (roughly chopped)

turmeric

paprika

cumin

chopped vegetables such as carrot, kumara, cauliflower, courgette, green beans, eggplant, mushrooms.

1 can tomatoes

1 can lentils (or cooked dried lentils)

Fry onions, garlic and celery in vegetable oil until slightly soft. Add spices and hardest vegetables (e.g. carrot and kumara) and cook for a few minutes stirring frequently. Add all vegetables gradually, from hardest to softest, stirring occasionally until the medium vegetables (courgette) are just tender. Add tomatoes and lentils. Simmer until heated through and serve.

June Fallen

TE PO

AT NELSON CENTRAL SCHOOL

Kia ora koutou, I started at Nelson Central as a student in 1986 and was in the first whanau class (bi-lingual unit) which began in 1988. I have grown up around Nelson and have had a lot of my family come through the school too. I used to bus to school, but once we moved up The Brook it was only a quick walk down the road.

The school environment hasn't changed too much. There are still the famous lime trees out the front and apart from a few new upgrades and classrooms, the school still looks pretty much the same as when I was a student here. I am now a teacher at this school in Te Pouahi, and I love being able to say to my students 'When I went to this school...' They love hearing about the two teachers that were here when I was a child, who are still here today. Nelson Central School is so special that some people just don't want to leave!

My daughter Ana now comes to Nelson Central. She is half Tongan and half Maori and she enjoys many types of Maori kai. Ana is able to make her own doughboys to put inside a boil-up, she also loves fried bread with butter and golden syrup, hangi and bully beef stew. One of her favourite Islander dishes is her dad's chop suey, which she can't wait to cook for herself one day, though this is rather different from the pork and puha boil-ups that Mum makes.

Erina Tuhakaraina

TONGAN CHOP SUEY WITH TARO

500ml soy sauce
500g mixed vegetables
1 bag of vermicelli
1 clove of garlic
1 clove of ginger
600g pork or chicken

Place vermicelli into a bowl with boiled water, cover and set aside.

Cut the meat into small, edible portions, put into pot with a cup of water and cook until meat is brown and tender.

Dice ginger and garlic finely and add to cooked meat and stir, followed by mixed vegetables.

Drain off any water in the vermicelli bowl, add to the ingredients in the pot and stir. Add soy sauce while continuing to stir, until the sauce has spread right through the food. Leave to simmer for 5 minutes before serving.

Chop suey can be served with rice, manioke (tapioca) or taro. Taro can be cooked like potatoes. To add a bit of flavour, make a sauce to cover taro once it is cooked. For the sauce, warm some (about 250ml) cream until hot, add a sachet of chicken soup powder and combine. Bring gently to boil then turn on low and simmer. Once ready, pour over cut up taro and serve.

From the Port Hills (above) looking west over Haulashore Island to Mt. Arthur and the Western Ranges, and a 180˚ turn (below) to the east - with Fringed Hill and the Grampians.

FIFESHIRE HOUSE

Fifeshire House, standing on Trafalgar Square, is one of Nelson's many heritage buildings noted for its historical, architectural and cultural significance. Raglan Brewery was established in 1855 on the site now occupied by the Rutherford Hotel and Fifeshire House. The brewery was taken over in 1859 by Mr Charles Harley, who renamed it Harley and Sons and over the years Harley and Sons became well respected brewers, achieving both local and international acclaim. The Harley family have long been a respected name in the area, and a large part of Nelson's heritage, actively shaping the Nelson that we live in today. Joseph Auty Harley was mayor of Nelson from 1899 to 1901, as was Charles John Harley from 1915 to 1917 and finally Joseph Auty Harley (the second) from 1947 to 1956.

In the early 1900s the Harley family built Raglan Villa near the brewery, with a garden transformed from an overgrown paddock into a beautiful landscape of lillies, ferns and dahlias. Raglan Villa became well known throughout Nelson as being a warm, inviting place where informal gatherings, and formal dinners were often held.

The villa remained a residence until the 1970s, when it became a community centre for the arts and other organisations. In 1987 Fifeshire FM moved into the villa, and made minor alterations to accommodate broadcasting studios and offices, carefully keeping the late Victorian style of the building. It then became known locally as Fifeshire House. Today Fifeshire House is the proud home of MediaWorks Nelson and is a vital part of the local community, where the family atmosphere that has long been a part of the history of this site, still remains today.

Some people believe that Fifeshire House is haunted by a friendly ghost called Violet, who was a maid in the house many years ago. There are a number of stories about Violet, but with no records to substantiate any of the speculation into fact, perhaps you will have to visit Fifeshire House and see for yourself. These recipes are examples of what might have been served from the Harley kitchen by a maid such as Violet, making the most of what was available, including the nearby family brewery, on one of the Harleys' many social occasions.

Rob Brown

House in Church Street. The Nelson Provincial Museum, F N Jones Collection: 310408

HARLEY'S ALE AND PIGEON PIE

This pie can be made in one large baking dish or six ramekins. Cooking time 2 hours 45 minutes.

700g pigeon meat – off the bone (or any poultry or red meat, if preferred)

2 tsp (heaped) plain flour (seasoned with salt and pepper)

oil or butter

1 onion (chopped)

1 carrot

4 sticks of celery

1 small handful of fresh herbs (rosemary, thyme or bay leaf)

1 (500ml) bottle of Ale (or any beer you prefer - if using red meat, use a darker beer)

800g (2 cans) chopped tomatoes

500g puff pastry

1 egg (lightly beaten)

Coat meat with the flour.

Brown the meat in oil or butter, add onion and fry for a further minute, add chopped celery, carrot and herbs and continue to fry for a further 5 minutes.

Add the beer and tinned tomatoes and bring to the boil. Stir well, then simmer for two hours or until the meat is tender.

Preheat the oven to 190°C.

Roll out pastry and line your baking dish(es), ensuring the pastry over-hangs the edge of the dish, and set aside enough pastry for the top of the pie. Put the meat filling into pie cases. Brush the rims of dish(es) with egg, then place the pastry on top, pinching the edges to ensure a seal is made in your pie. Lightly score the top of the pie and brush with the remainder of the egg.

Place on a baking tray (in case the filling overflows) and bake in the middle of the oven for 45 minutes until golden.

To serve, cut a small hole in the top and pour over Violet's Worcestershire Sauce (made ahead of time).

VIOLET'S WORCESTERSHIRE SAUCE

2 litres malt vinegar

4 cloves garlic

3 Tbsp common salt

140g (1/3 tin) treacle

1 tsp cayenne pepper

2 Tbsp ground cloves

½ cup plain flour

Add all ingredients together in a large pot, bring to boil and keep boiling for 30 minutes. Add ½ cup of flour mixed with cold vinegar to thicken. Bring to boil again, then strain and bottle. Cap when cold.

Fifeshire Rock

PORK AND PUHA

Kia ora koutou. My children all went to Nelson Central School, in the whanau class from 1988 to 2006. I now have a granddaughter at the school and some more grandchildren on their way there. A dish I liked to cook for my children while they were growing up was a boil-up, which they still all enjoy today.

A unique Maori dish is the boil-up. A meal cooked in one pot. Meat such as pork bones, vegetables including kumara, pumpkin and potatoes, puha (thistle that grows in the garden) or watakihi watercress (grows in the creek). Doughboys, also known as 'dumplings', can be added too. Base the amount of ingredients on how many people you are cooking for. A larger amount means the pot can be reheated the following day and for some reason it tastes even more delicious!

big bunch of puha or watakihi
pork bones
kumara (sweet potato) peeled
potato, peeled
pumpkin, peeled and deseeded
water to cover the pork bones
salt to taste

Put the pork bones into a large pot, salt and bring to the boil then turn on to medium for about an hour. Clean the puha or watakihi under running water, removing any discoloured leaves or additional weeds and then compress with your hands to remove the sour juices (dark green colour) to make sure the puha is going to be sweet and tasty.

Place the puha in the pot with the pork bones, add the vegetables and press down into the pot, covering the vegetables with the juice. Leave the lid off the pot. When the vegetables are nearly cooked, add the doughboys and continue cooking for another half an hour.

Serve with Maori bread (rewana or fried bread).

Sandy Tuhakaraina

‘In 1975 Margareta and I made the risky decision that I would earn my living as a writer. We arrived in Nelson and for several years were church-mouse poor, so buying cheap food was a necessity. We soon discovered that the area was rich in things that grow and that pick-your-own lowered costs even further.’

Maurice Gee

STONEGRILL
DINING
OF NELSON

NASI GORENG

When Mackensey was very young, she would ask me to cook this, and still does. She just loves Nasi Goreng but only the way I make it! Watch out though, make sure your rangehood is on or windows are open as the trasi has a "different" sort of smell...

2 medium onions
1 tsp crushed garlic
½ tsp trasi (dried shrimp paste)
1 tsp coriander
1 tsp cumin
¼ tsp laos powder
1 tsp brown sugar
sambal ulek, or finely chopped chillies (optional)
500g chicken, pork or beef cut into slices or cubes
250g shrimps or prawns
peanut oil for cooking
4 cups of cold cooked rice (not sticky rice)
kecap manis (sweet soy sauce)
krupuk udang (shrimp crackers)

Garnish

2-3 eggs
roasted peanuts
cucumber

Chop onions roughly and put in a food processor with the garlic, spices and sugar. Blend to a paste.

Heat about 3 Tbsp of oil in a large frying pan or wok and fry blended ingredients until cooked. Add the meat and when almost fully cooked add the shrimp or prawns. Stir constantly to avoid it sticking. Add a little more oil and add the rice, tossing to mix in well. Just before serving drizzle over a little kecap manis.

Garnish with strips of omelette, roasted peanuts, freshly cut strips of cucumber and freshly cooked krupuk udang. More kecap manis can be added if necessary.

The omelette can be made easily by beating 2 or 3 eggs with salt and pepper and frying in a little oil. Do not fold the omelette, just cook on low until cooked through.

Carol, John and Mackensey Wyllie (and Elysia and Kasey)

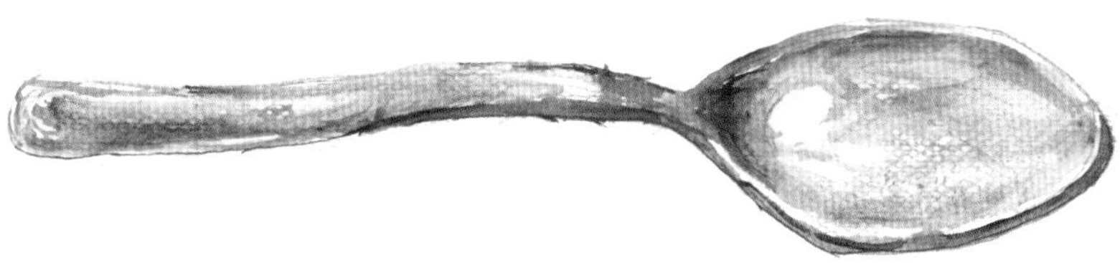

CAMBODIAN CHICKEN MANGO AND CASHEW STIR-FRY

This quick and easy recipe is from *The Best of Friends* cookbook. Friends The Restaurant, Phnom Penh, was part of Mith Samlanh, a child-centred programme committed to the Convention of the Rights of the Child, offering food, shelter, medical care, training and education for over 1,800 homeless or abandoned children daily.

Cooking this meal reminds me of the hard work being done to give Cambodian street children hope and opportunity. Serves 4

2 Tbsp vegetable oil

2 garlic cloves, chopped

1 medium white onion, chopped

200g mushrooms, diced

600g skinless, boneless chicken, sliced

2 Tbsp dry white wine

2 Tbsp oyster sauce

1 tsp cornflour

1½ cups chicken stock

1 tsp brown sugar

2 mangoes, not too ripe, peeled and sliced into 1cm thick pieces

½ cup roasted cashew nuts, unsalted

salt and pepper to taste

spring onions, sliced

Heat vegetable oil in large frying pan or wok. Add garlic and onion, fry until fragrance is released. Add mushrooms, fry until browned. Add chicken and fry for 2 minutes. Add wine, oyster sauce, and sauté.

Add cornflour to the chicken stock, then add to chicken mixture and fry for 1 minute.

Add sugar, mangoes, cashew nuts, salt and pepper, mix and fry for 1 minute.

Serve garnished with spring onions.

Tracy Watkin

SMOKED CHILLI CHICKEN

I enjoy preparing smoked chilli chicken as an alternative to a barbecue, the long cooking time allowing for a generous wine tasting session prior to dining. The chilli flavour that comes through in this recipe fills and warms your cheeks from the inside. It is flexible enough to vary the quantities listed to cater for a wide range of preferences. You can add to either the brine or the rub to create the flavours that you desire. You will need a 'smoker' to cook this though!

Brine

2 Tbsp salt

1 Tbsp brown sugar

3 litres of water, or enough to cover chicken

Chicken chilli rub

Adapted from traditional recipes used for smoking other meats.

1 tsp cayenne

1 tsp chilli powder

¼ Tbsp cumin

2 tsp garlic powder

1 tsp mustard powder

1 tsp onion salt

2 tsp paprika

Place a whole chicken in brine solution for 4 hours.

Remove and allow to drain for 1 hour and dry with paper towels.

Mix ingredients for the rub in a small bowl and apply rub all over chicken, inside and out, then allow chicken to sit for 2 hours.

Preheat upright smoker to 360°C.

Place chicken in middle layer of smoker and allow to cook for 2½ to 3 hours or until cooked.

Paul Potaka (Principal, Nelson Central School)

ROASTED PORTUGUESE CHICKEN

1.6 kg chicken or chicken joints
3 cloves crushed garlic
2 tsp salt
½ cup lemon juice
2 Tbsp olive oil
1 Tbsp dried or fresh oregano
2 Tbsp brown sugar
2 Tbsp paprika
chilli powder to taste
ovenproof dish with lid

If using a whole chicken, butterfly and prick it all over with a fork first.

Mix all ingredients together.

Place chicken in an oven proof dish and spread the mixture all over the chicken. Leave to marinate for at least one hour.

Place on middle shelf of oven set to 200°C for at least 40 minutes, or until brown and juices run clear.

Remove chicken from dish and keep warm, use cornflour or flour to thicken juice.

Return chicken to dish and baste with juice just before serving.

Lovely served with rice and green vegetables.

All ingredients can be adjusted to liking, smoked paprika works really well too.

Choi Fu

Nelson Central School Matariki hangi

TRADE

CHICKEN TAGINE WITH APRICOTS AND ALMONDS

Having seen and admired tagines while travelling, I desperately wanted one for its art and cultural value. Fortunately it also has a really practical application and I have come to enjoy the flavours and aromas that can be created in the tagine. This recipe has been adapted from a long lost source and can be enjoyed anytime. (A heavy casserole dish will suffice if you don't have a tagine.)

6-8 portions of chicken
½ tsp ground black pepper
1 tsp ground ginger
½ tsp turmeric
½ tsp salt
4 Tbsp olive oil
1 Tbsp butter
2-3 medium onions sliced thickly
4 cloves garlic, peeled and crushed
6 stalks fresh coriander
½ cup white wine
2 Tbsp honey
½ cup water
1 cinnamon stick
½ cup dried apricots
½ cup blanched almonds
⅓ cup chopped parsley

Mix in a large bowl; black pepper, ginger, turmeric, ¼ tsp salt and 2 Tbsp of olive oil. Rub mixture into chicken pieces. Heat butter and 2 Tbsp of olive oil in a heavy pan and brown chicken.

Transfer browned chicken to tagine.

Add onion and remaining salt and cook uncovered for 5-8 minutes. Add garlic and cook for 3 minutes, stirring occasionally.

Tie coriander into a bundle and add to the tagine along with ½ cup wine.

Reduce heat and simmer covered for 1½ hours or until cooked.

Bring honey, water, cinnamon stick and apricots to boil in a small pot.

Reduce heat and simmer, uncovered, until apricots are tender.

Cook almonds in a small pan over a moderate heat but don't burn them!

Remove and place on paper towel to drain.

Before chicken is cooked, discard coriander and cinnamon stick and add apricot mixture to tagine for last 2-3 minutes of cooking time. Simmer to reduce liquid, add almonds and serve with chopped parsley.

Paul Potaka (Principal, Nelson Central School)

Emile Henry
FRANCE

LAMB SHANKS WITH GARLIC AND MASH

This hearty meal keeps my boys happy every time. Food for the soul.

8 lamb shanks
4 heads of garlic
olive oil
2 Tbsp flour
2 Tbsp tomato paste
1 tsp brown sugar
1½ cups red wine
3 cups liquid beef stock
½ cup fresh rosemary chopped

Place flour in plastic bowl with salt and pepper, add shanks and lightly cover.

Heat oil in a large, heavy based pan and brown shanks in batches.

Transfer shanks to a large baking dish and add garlic, halved crosswise.

Discard fat from pan, add tomato paste and cook gently for one minute, then add brown sugar, red wine, stock and rosemary.

Bring to a fast simmer, stir to lift sediments from the bottom of pan.

Pour over shanks, cover with foil and bake gently at 180°C for at least 2 hours, or until meat is falling off the bone. Check regularly to ensure liquid hasn't evaporated and add more stock if necessary.

Serve with mashed spuds and greens such as steamed green beans, asparagus and bok choy.

Mash

7-8 medium potatoes
2-3 Tbsp butter
¼ cup hot milk or cream

Peel and cut potatoes into chunks. Boil in salted water until tender. Drain thoroughly.

Place back on low heat to evaporate moisture briefly. Then, using a masher, mash and then add butter and hot milk or cream.

Mix until creamy and smooth. Season with salt and pepper.

Alex Chisnall

THE SATURDAY MARKET

Locals love to bang on about how Nelson's Saturday market is noisy, friendly, alive and colourful; a vibrant multi-cultural hub of the local community, yada yada yada, and fair enough. It's true. But if I'm honest, the main reason I love this place is that it keeps me from getting too thin. Every Saturday morning I wander down there, rain or shine, ignoring all the tourist trap craft stalls and head straight for the tucker.

I queue alongside a gaggle of ravenous ex-pat Germans to buy the nation's best bratwurst from Doris's German small-goods stall. I stock up on fresh chorizo from George, the lovely Portuguese guy, and cadge a few morsels of his sherry-roasted pork. I invest in a slab of smoked mackerel from the Mapua Wharf Smokehouse stall, some creamy white Mt. Crusader sheep's cheese from the Neudorf Dairy stall and a loaf of still-warm sourdough from Tozzetti Panetteria. I buy half a kilo of wild-shot Marlborough goat meat so I can satisfy my goat curry addiction later in the week, and stock up on seasonal veges from the sunburnt market gardener geezer with the dubious leather shorts. On the rare occasion that I'm hung over, I hoe into a big bowl of curative Tom Yum soup from the Thai stall, followed by a long black from Jason's coffee cart, which dishes out reliably powerful jolts of caffeine to a life-affirming soundtrack of 70's funk and 80's hip hop.

It's a market that can be relied upon to meet one's deepest needs, whether culinary or cultural. One scorching day last summer, some clear-eyed hippies at the organic nursery stall sold me a dozen heirloom eggplant seedlings and just five minutes later, an aging punk sold me a scratchy old vinyl copy of the "Give 'Em Enough Rope" LP by The Clash. That's a proper market, that is.

Grant Smithies

A NELSON SPIN ON JAMAICAN GOAT CURRY

Buy a packet of diced wild goat from the Nelson market. Drain meat, pat dry with paper towels, then roll in a bowl with few tablespoons of hot curry powder (Vencat "Hot" is good, or use your own blend), making sure the dry spices coat each cube of meat. Set aside in fridge for a couple of hours.

Preheat oven to around 120° C.

In a cast-iron pot with close-fitting lid, sweat off one large finely-diced onion until soft but not browned. Add one or two red capsicums cut into large chunks. Finely dice two fresh chillies (or dried) and more if you like it hot, four cloves of garlic, a thumb-sized lump of peeled root ginger, and a few sprigs of thyme. Add to pot.

Add three or four diced fresh tomatoes, or half a tin of chopped tomatoes. Cook a few minutes until pulpy. Add a big pinch of salt, and a can of full-fat coconut cream. Turn off heat and set aside.

In a hot frying pan, fry off the spice-covered diced goat in small batches until it has some good colour, being careful not to crowd the pan, otherwise it will stew rather than brown. Add each batch to pot containing coconut cream mixture.

When all of the goat is browned off, heat up coconut/goat mixture on stovetop until bubbling, then put on lid and slide pot into the preheated oven.

Every 15 minutes or so, slide out pot, take off lid and give it a stir. After about 45 minutes, meat will be starting to soften. At this point, peel and dice a kumara into roughly 2cm square chunks and add to pot (if added earlier, it will totally dissolve). If you have no kumara, pumpkin is also delicious. Cook for a further 20 minutes or so in the oven with the lid on, stirring occasionally, until meat is tender and kumara/pumpkin is cooked.

You'll know it's nearly done when a little oil from the meat and coconut cream rises to the surface, which you stir back through before serving. Remove from oven, serve over rice, sprinkled with chopped coriander. Great with a cold beer and a soundtrack of loud, bass-heavy music from Kingston, Jamaica.

Grant Smithies

Digital Copy Centre
& Design Studio
Nelson
Potters

MILD BEEF CURRY

This recipe makes a curry that's spicy, but not hot so even our kids like it. It makes a big curry, enough for leftovers the next day.

1 Tbsp plain cooking oil
1kg diced beef (any stewing cut will do)
2 onions, chopped
2 cloves garlic, crushed
2 green chillies (optional)
1 Tbsp grated fresh ginger
1½ tsp turmeric
1 tsp ground cumin
1 Tbsp ground coriander
1 tsp chilli powder (optional)
1 tsp salt
400g can of crushed tomatoes
400ml can of light coconut cream
2 large potatoes
fresh coriander, for serving

Heat the oil in a pan and brown the meat in small batches. Remove from the pan and set aside. Cook the onions in the same pan until they are soft, then add the garlic, chilli, cumin, ginger, turmeric, coriander, and chilli powder. Return the meat to the pan and stir until coated with the spices. Add the salt, tomatoes, and coconut cream and bring to a simmer. Cover and cook over a low heat for 2 hours, until the meat is tender. Add the diced potato, cover again, and cook for another 20 minutes until the potato is cooked. Serve with rice. Fresh coriander on top is nice, if you have some.

Jenny Smith

FRIKADELLEN *German oven meatballs*

5 slices white toast bread
3 chopped onions (or fewer, to taste)
2 cups parsley (flat is best)
1kg beef mince (or half beef and half pork mince)
3 eggs
3 Tbsp mustard
salt and pepper to season

Preheat oven to 225°C and line a baking dish with baking paper.

Cover the bread with water, then squeeze tightly to remove liquid.

Mix all ingredients together and make 18 meatballs.

Bake for 10 minutes, turn meatballs over and bake for a further 10 minutes.

Martina Friedrich

NEW ZEALAND PREMIUM QUALITY
NEW ZEALAND PREMIUM QUALITY
PALM
CORNED BE
WITH JUICES
PRODUCT OF NEW ZEALAND
5
4
1

MACKIE STEW

This is a family recipe that has been lovingly passed down through the Mackie Clan in Takahiwai. It is an art and no thickening should be used. Whanau love it and new additions to the family have pretended to love it..but have eventually come around to the 'stew side'. We have been heard to say 'no, this is Mackie stew not bullybeef stew'. My Nana Connie would cook it for us and now my mum cooks it on request.

1 tin of corned beef, cut into chunks

2 medium white onions, diced.

3 carrots (optional) peeled, halved lengthwise and cut into half rounds

6 potatoes medium size, peeled and diced.

Hints

Corned Beef. Very pricey now but try to choose a reputable brand with minimum fat.

Onions. When cooked should melt into the stew.

Carrots. Should be small or thinly sliced as they must cook at the same time as potatoes.

Potatoes. Use the potatoes that mush easy but also have some integrity.

Place potatoes, carrots and onions into pot.

Cover with water, salt water. Water should just cover potatoes.

Bring to a simmer and cook until the potatoes, onion and carrots are cooked. Carrots are not falling apart, potatoes slightly mushed bit still have some substance and onions are transparent.

Fold-stir the stew to stop the stew from mushing and the bottom of pot catching.

Add corned beef. Make sure that corned beef is gently stirred through mixture. Simmer.

The potato should thicken the stew. Add a bit of water if too thick. Taste test for salt levels.

For flash food look, add parsley

Serve with fried bread. If any stew is left over, serve on or beside toast for supper or breakfast.

Carly Ave

NMIT

FOOD CULTURE

(The Celebration of Mediterranean Ingredients)

Right across from Central School is the NMIT Hospitality and Wellbeing Building. When you take a walk down Nile Street you can look through the floor to ceiling windows and see chefs busy at work, all in crisp white hats, sometimes with a bright coloured scarf adding a splash of colour to the monochrome vision. At night, with the lights on, it is a fabulous bright sight, stainless steel gleaming and pots steaming. It is excellent to know that hard at work are the fledgling leaders of Nelson food culture.

Next door to the kitchens is the Rata Room, the quirky modern NMIT restaurant with the big horseshoe bar, where these budding chefs create food for the people of Nelson to sample, served by front of house students who are learning the craft of being a maitre'd and helping to raise the service standards in Nelson's busy restaurant scene.

The NMIT culinary and food and beverage tutors inspire the students to achieve greatness and contribute to developing Nelson's regional cuisine. There is a strong sense of making the most of the food produced locally, linking it with place and the seasons, and knowing that it tastes better, has richer flavours and more intense aromas.

Nelson is increasingly recognised as a true Mediterranean food bowl and NMIT chef students also have the opportunity to gain a deeper insight into it by specialising in Italian regional gastronomy through a link with Academia Barilla in Parma, Italy. Chef tutor James Perry is a local expert and he imparts the wisdom the Italians have developed over centuries, an understanding of the deep link between food and culture and how that translates to what is presented on the plate.

Elizabeth Latham

TORTELLI DI ERBETTE

(Silver beet and ricotta stuffed ravioli) Serves 4.

The filling

1 bunch silver beet, about 6 large leaves

600g ricotta cheese

50g grated parmigiano reggiano cheese

¼ onion finely chopped

25g butter

1 egg

pinch of nutmeg

salt

For pasta

400g 00 flour- available from 'Prego' (Mediterranean Foods)

2 eggs

water

Sauce

50g butter

grated parmigiano reggiano cheese

Serve with

torn sage leaves

slow roasted cherry tomatoes

To make the filling: Clean the silver beet, remove the 'ribs' and put into a saucepan with a little water to stop the silver beet from sticking. Put the lid on the pot and cook over gentle heat until the silver beet has wilted.

Turn off the heat and put the silver beet into a sieve to drain and cool. When cool squeeze out the moisture. Mix together the ricotta and the parmigiano reggiano cheese. Chop the onion finely and sauté in a little butter, chop the silver beet finely and add to the onion. Cool the mixture, then add the beaten egg, a pinch of salt and a pinch of freshly grated nutmeg. Mix the cheeses and silver beet together.

To make the pasta dough: Mix together the flour, egg and as much water as necessary to make a dough that holds together well and is firm and dry. Knead for about 10 minutes until it is smooth and elastic. Roll out as thin as possible either by hand or using a pasta machine. You need the dough to be large enough to make 24 individual tortelli. About 1m by 200mm wide (the width of the pasta machine).

Putting it together: Onto the dough, place 1 tablespoon dollops of the ricotta mixture over half of the dough, each spoonful spaced about 5 cm apart. Fold the other half of the sheet over and press around the cheese mixture. Cut into rectangles about 60mm by 80mm in size, preferably using a pasta cutter. Close the edges by pressing with the tip of a fork.

Cook the tortelli in well-salted water, in a large pasta pot for 15 minutes, drain well. Reserve a little of the pasta water.

In a large pan melt the butter and add the cooked tortelli, toss gently. Add a ladle full of the pasta water to add starch to the sauce. Sprinkle with the cheese and torn sage leaves that have been quickly sautéed in some extra virgin olive oil, then drained on a paper towel. Serve immediately with cherry tomatoes that have been sliced in half, drizzled with extra virgin olive oil, sea salt and freshly ground black pepper and cooked in a slow oven 130°C for 1 hour. The tomatoes are a great garnish and add an excellent taste burst.

James Perry and Academia Barilla

BEEF AND BEANS WITH PASTA

Based on a recipe from Nigella Lawson, this makes a soupy bowl of pasta and is very quick, easy and delicious. Known as macaroni mix-up in our house.

1 onion
1 clove of garlic
1 carrot
½ stick of celery
1-2 Tbsp olive oil
250g minced beef
1 litre stock
400g tinned tomatoes
2 Tbsp red wine
250g macaroni or pasta of choice
400g tin beans (red kidney or cannellini)
parmesan cheese

Whizz up the onion, garlic, carrot and celery in a food processor. (Replace celery with extra carrot if you like.) Fry in the oil for 5 minutes. Add the beef and cook until browned.

Add the tinned tomatoes, stock, wine and bring to the boil.

Add the macaroni and cook uncovered for 18-20 minutes.

Add the beans towards the end of cooking.

Season and serve in bowls with lots of grated parmesan.

Sarah Challenger

FILLET OF BEEF

Take a fillet of beef, stab holes in the meat and poke in small pieces of garlic. Smear with good quality Dijon or French mustard. Pour enough olive oil to coat the bottom of a metal baking dish. Place beef in pan and overlay with strips of streaky bacon. Surround beef with button mushrooms. Bake in hot oven for about 30 minutes depending on size of fillet. Rest before serving with your favourite vegetables.

EAT

Nelson Central School
Board of Trustees

'A visitor to New Zealand once asked me,'What does that ship carry?'He was pointing to one of the enormous and slightly ridiculous looking floating blocks with a picture of a dolphin on the side of it.'Oh that one, yes, full of dolphins. We like to eat on them on toast here.' He was appalled! Anyway, I set him straight, and then I served him his lunch - something on toast probably.'

Daniel Monopoli

FROM STROMBOLI TO NELSON

From early in the 20th Century there was significant Italian migration to the top of the South Island. Best known are the Italian tomato growers who settled and prospered in The Wood, in central Nelson, and by the 1950s numbered 40-50 families. Undoubtedly their passionate culture of food spread its influence out into the Nelson community.

Further afield, the Russo and Moleta cousins from the tiny island of Stromboli, off Sicily, carved out a farm at Waitai on D'Urville Island. The farm stayed in the Moleta family until 1999. The story of Angelina and Vincenzo Moleta is told in the acclaimed *Angelina: From Stromboli to D'Urville Island*, by their grandson Gerard Hindmarsh. In it he beautifully evokes Vincenzo's memories of his family kitchen.

'I can see still my Mumma's apron, all covered in handprints of flour from her big day in the kitchen. She is chatting excitedly as she carries over endless dishes, and every dish she puts down hits us right in our noses. Balsamic vinegar, crushed oregano, basil, tomato, focaccia bread, delicious freshly baked pesce. Each dish cuts down our conversations. As Mumma puts that last dish on table, there's not one word in the room. Our noses just call us to dinner.

Right in the middle of our big table is the biggest dish of pesce gnotta you'll ever see. Bartolo caught the swordfish off Punta d' 'I Chiappo the day before. The fish is baked with potatoes mixed with fresh herbs, vino, a handful of cappari, and swimming in a puree of the ripest plum tomatoes. Alongside is a big bowl of carciofuli chini, artichoke done in breadcrumbs. Mangiare di Stromboli – simple delicious food, like our lifestyle.'

Gerard Hindmarsh was given the following recipe by his mother Francesca, daughter of Angelina and Vincenzo. Clearly it has been modified for life in New Zealand, as they had no beef cattle on Stromboli.

Robbie Burton

MUMA'S GOURMET MEAT BALLS

Meatballs

500g beef mince, high grade (serves six)

1 medium sized farm egg

1 cup of fresh breadcrumbs

2 cloves of garlic, finely diced

1 small sprig finely chopped fresh parsley

Sauce

½kg tomatoes cut open (or one tin/small jar of concentrate)

15 leaves of fresh basil, ripped apart by fingers - or dried basil to taste

5 cloves garlic, finely chopped

1 medium onion, finely chopped

bay leaves (half a dozen or so)

3 generous dollops of balsamic vinegar

good sprinkle of oregano

1 Tbsp runny farm honey or 1 tsp sugar

any red wine left over from last night

salt and pepper

Form the meatballs early (storing them uncooked for five hours in the fridge after forming them will bind them together). Mix mince, breadcrumbs, egg, diced garlic and parsley. Mix well and mould them with palms into balls.

Begin cooking at least two hours before you want to serve. First fry in hot oil the chopped onion and garlic. When well sautéed, roughly scrape them out into a bowl which contains the rest of the sauce ingredients, adding one cup or so of water and stir to mix well. Sear the meatballs in the pan, still well oiled, with the garlic and onion juice, and when they are thoroughly brown add the sauce which should just cover the meatballs. Simmer for around two hours, giving it a quick shake periodically to spread the flavours. Just before serving, increase heat and take off lid to let sauce thicken.

Serve piping hot over al dente pasta and sprinkle with gratings of parmesan.

Gerard Hindmarsh

Angelina and Vincenzo Moleta

SPAGHETTI ALLA CARBONARA

One of the most common dishes in Italy, my own country. From north to south, every single family knows how to make it. It's fast and very yummy. Buon appetito. (Serves 4)

400g spaghetti (Barilla is the best pasta you can find easily in Nelson)
200g smoked bacon, chopped finely
4 eggs
1 onion, thinly sliced
olive oil
parmesan, fistful
1 glass of red wine
salt and pepper

The Sauce

In a bowl, beat the eggs together: 3 yolks and only 1 whole egg. The proportion is very important; so if you have 5 people, you will use 5 eggs (one egg each), but it will be 4 yolks and only one whole egg. Add a fistful of grated Parmesan, salt and pepper. Mix all the ingredients together to make a cream.

Meanwhile

Put a couple of spoons of olive oil in a pan. Add the onion and fry until golden. Add the bacon and fry until it becomes a little bit crispy. Add the wine and cook for few minutes. The wine must evaporate completely and be absorbed by the onion and bacon.

It shouldn't be too dry....but, at the same time, not too liquid.

Cooking the Pasta

When you prepare pasta, one of the most important secrets is to boil it in a very big pot. This pot must be almost full of water (it will take 10-15 minutes before the water boils). Put in a handful of salt. When the water boils, put the spaghetti into the pot and mix with a fork (otherwise it will stick together).

For cooking times, follow the instructions on the pasta box. Drain the pasta when ready, not overcooked. Put the pasta immediately into the bowl with the egg sauce. Add the onion and bacon to the pasta (they also must be hot). Mix up all together and it's ready to be eaten!

Francesca Willis

Former NCS student's Urban Art as part of Nelson's Urban Art Festival

RUBY'S LAST SUPPER *(Salmon fettuccine fit for a dog)*

This recipe has been a favourite of Ian and mine since I first discovered it in a pasta recipe book about 10 years ago. It was sweet and sour anything before that, and like most people lamb shanks since! Living at St Arnaud, it is good to have something special to serve up at a moment's notice if friends stay unexpectedly for dinner.

As long as you have the three main ingredients: smoked salmon, fettuccine and the carton of lite cream, you are nearly there. I buy sun-dried tomatoes and capers in bulk from Prego on Halifax Street, so I always have them on hand.

Ruby, our 15 year old Labrador just loved this dish and would raise her nose to the aroma of the salmon as it sizzled in a pan. Even if we had people for dinner I would always save a little for Ruby. She would nudge my elbow as I sat in a chair with a bowl of salmon fettuccine giving me the 'Don't Forget Me' look of appeal. After she became ill and lost her appetite I'd wave a bowl of salmon fettuccine under her nose which aroused her interest. I could see the gleam come back and she'd start salivating. Yes, life was still worth living, there was salmon and pasta for dinner.

200g Marlborough Wood Smoked Salmon, (can otherwise be a glazed fillet or pkt of salmon leaves)

400g fresh fettuccine (for four servings)

250ml carton of lite cream

1-2 tsp whole seed mustard

2 Tbsp of butter melted in the pan

½ cup of sun dried tomatoes (cut into quarters or strips, not too small)

2-3 Tbsp capers or caper berries (plus juice for a piquant flavour)

pepper and salt to taste

juice of a lemon or lime

spring onions or chives (chopped) to decorate

Melt the butter in a frying pan. Add 1-2 Tbsp of mustard - mixing with the melted butter.

Add the carton of lite cream to heat and then the salmon (bite sized pieces), being careful not to boil. Add the sun-dried tomatoes and caper berries (and juice if desired).

Cook the fettuccine, drain and tip into a shallow, wide pasta dish or bowl.

Pour the salmon mixture on the top of the fettuccine (it mixes through as people serve it to their plates).

Squeeze the juice of half the lemon over main dish and chop the rest into wedges as garnish and for individuals who like more lemon.

Sprinkle with the chopped spring onions or chives.
Serve immediately.

Eileen Street

Take 2 on SALMON FETTUCCINE

This is quick, easy and delicious.

2 Tbsp butter

2 Tbsp flour

pinch salt

¼ cup milk

2 cloves crushed garlic

1 Tbsp fish sauce in ½ cup water

2 Tbsp grated parmesan cheese

210g salmon (3 x steaks- cooked first in microwave, remove bones and reserve juice)

4 spring onions, finely chopped

400g fresh fettuccine

parsley sprigs for garnishing

cracked pepper

Melt butter in frypan, stir in flour and cook until mixture bubbles.

Add garlic and salt and then fish stock in water slowly, stirring until smooth.

Gently heat until thick, then add milk and parmesan cheese until a medium thickness.

Add spring onions, salmon and reserved juice.

Cook fettuccine and drain into large serving bowl and toss salmon mixture through. Garnish with parsley sprigs. Season with cracked pepper.

Kay McQuire

TRADITIONAL ENGLISH FISHCAKES

Audible groans were commonplace in our house when inquiries as to what was for dinner were met with 'fish.' Children of a deep sea Skipper, it featured regularly on the menu. This child and budget-friendly dish followed our family from Hull, in the north-east of England and remains a firm favourite, especially when accompanied by mushy peas. (Makes 8 large fishcakes)

1.2kg potatoes (variety suited to mashing)

400g fresh fish (or tinned salmon, tuna - but do try for fresh)

3 Tbsp olive oil

1 egg beaten

salt to taste

handful of fresh herbs finely chopped or ½ tsp dried sage

½ cup plain or rice flour (reserve for coating fishcakes)

2 Tbsp oil (for frying fishcakes)

Peel, boil and mash potatoes. Allow to cool slightly.

Poach or bake fish and then flake. Add fish and remaining ingredients (except flour) and mix well. Shape into round patties (1 inch thick). Coat patties in flour.

Oil the frypan and gently brown fishcakes both sides.

See my recipe for Mam's Mushy Peas (p.61) to go with these.

Deb Hardcastle

JAPANESE FOOD ON NEW ZEALAND POTTERY

When my partner Chris and I travel, we like to eat! And with every trip away, there's always another recipe or two that get added to my precious, stained and tatty A4 folder. Our trip to Japan in 2007, however, was quite different: it wasn't just about accumulating recipes, it ended up having a profound impact on the way we eat.

I knew very little about Japan, but Chris's family has a strong connection. They lived there in 1969/70 while his dad, Dr Ivan Skinner, the revered father of Base Isolation, was working for UNESCO. He headed up a team of Japanese and international scientists who were developing buildings which would survive earthquakes. The family fell in love with Japan, its culture and its food. Long before it was fashionable, the Skinners were sitting down to sushi, miso and green tea, with a container full of chopsticks on the bench. Even today, when he goes to an Italian restaurant to eat pasta, Chris still asks if they have chopsticks. And that's why we ended up choosing Japan for a holiday, and to make it really special, it was the first time Chris had been back since he was sixteen.

I think you have to experience Japanese food before you can cook it yourself. The recipe books can be a mysterious maze of unfamiliar ingredients, techniques and equipment. It's hard to tell what the food should look like, taste like, what its texture should be, and how it should be laid out. I used to play a game of 'try to identify what ingredients have been used'. It was a mixed bag of success and failure – there were too many ingredients I'd never heard of, never tasted in my life or could not imagine being used that way. Like the sweet red filling of the doughy bun, hot out of the oven from a Tokyo street-vendor – what was that? It turned out to be anko, or sweetened red kidney bean paste - I thought kidney beans were supposed to be savoury!

When we came home, the first thing I did was pick up the recipe book which Chris's sister had given me for Christmas. Now it started to make sense. One dish I had eaten in Japan, a savoury custard with weird flavours, had left me stumped. But I discovered the recipe in my book and it turned out to be made of dashi (fish) stock and egg. And when I came to cook it, because I'd tasted it already I discovered that it is the little touches that make all the difference. I only use tiny amounts of smoked chicken or fish, mushroom, spring onion, capsicum, and I know now when I've over-baked it – the texture becomes rubbery instead of velvety.

I started to cook at least one Japanese meal a week, and also began to use a more Eastern presentation style, even with Western food. One of the things I noticed in Japan was that there was no 'dinner set' as such. Food is served in the vessel best suited for that item. The colour of the pottery, the shape of the plate, the texture of the dish - each is chosen to complement the food it is containing. It's usual to have several different styles of plates and bowls on the table at one time. When you're cooking Japanese food, you don't have to worry about everything matching, and I relish being able to just pick dishes and plates that best suit that particular food.

I grew up in the 60s and 70s loving our Nelson pottery, and it seems absolutely right to use this with Japanese food. We have delicately patterned black and white glazed bowls, perfect for rice and miso soup, by Sue Dasler. Our plain black sushi plates by Royce McGlashan work well with some quirky ones from Owen Barlett. Rose Griffin indulged me with a special run of small oblong plates so that each person can have a side dish with their own condiments: pickled vegetables, grated daikon radish (we grow our own), a gob of wasabi and maybe a slice of lemon to cleanse the palate between flavours. Our serving bowls are an eclectic mix, while each setting also has its own small bowl of dipping sauce – it's either soya or the sauce the Japanese go mad about, ponzu. I have two choices here. Royce McGlashan made a set of tiny bowls which are shaped like sea shells which are absolutely perfect, but occasionally I do go for the tiny, teal, Crown Lynn butter dishes which were once used in First Class on Air New Zealand. Crown Lynn Potteries also made our sensational sushi platter. Designed by David Jenkins, it was made especially for the Geyser Restaurant in the New Zealand Pavilion at the 1970 Osaka Expo. The platter has the motif of the legend of Maui, the palings of a pa fortification and mud pools in a strip from edge to edge. The fact that this dish came out of New Zealand in 1969 is an amazing part of our design history.

Annette Milligan

WHOLE STUFFED SALMON

This is our traditional Christmas dinner and is a really economical dish.

1 whole salmon

Stuffing
(even quantities of each, depending on size of the fish)

pesto

breadcrumbs

lightly toasted pine nuts

Run a sharp knife along the length of the fish to create a pocket above the bones. I make the opening much bigger to get more stuffing in.

Mix together the stuffing mixture. It can be dry and crumbly as it will soak up the juices from the salmon.

Wrap the whole fish in one piece of tinfoil. Roll over the edges of the tinfoil to seal.

Bake for 40 minutes at 180°C. The salmon should be slightly underdone.

Unroll the tinfoil and use spoons to gently lift and scrape the meat off the bones. You should be able leave the skeleton intact. Once one side is finished, flip the salmon over.

Serve the whole fish on a great big platter.

Keep the rest of the food light and simple as the salmon is so very rich in flavour. It goes well with breads, boiled potatoes, plain rice, salad, and plain vegetables.

It will last a few days in the fridge – we usually get several meals out of one salmon. Then I boil up the bones and skin to get a good rich stock to make a fish and vegetable stew.

Annette Milligan

SUSHI CONES

Sushi can be so complex that you can spend your whole life perfecting the technique. I like to keep it simple, especially when there are children or a big crowd. Everyone makes their own and chooses the ingredients they like. This is a great way to use up left-overs and it works really well with barbecued food too. Prepare the options keeping one thing to a bowl and chop the ingredients into strips (they're easier to manage). You need nori, which are sheets of green seaweed. Or use big lettuce leaves instead.

Fillings

Vegetables of choice, (3-4 types) usually raw, but some, like zucchini, are good grilled.

Meat/fish, (2 options) either cooked or smoked.

Rice, a big bowl, short grained because it sticks together better.

Sushi flavouring or rice vinegar, to tart the taste a bit.

Put all the ingredients on the table. Using your hands, roll a sheet of nori into a cone shape so it's closed at the bottom. Stuff a bit of rice in the bottom, and up one side of the cone. Add whatever ingredients you like into your cone, adding more rice and ingredients until you've filled the cone. Add a little wasabi and soya sauce if you like. Eat it right away - sushi is like a tomato sandwich - it's best when just made.

PONZU SAUCE

For dipping and especially good with salmon. Equal quantities of soya sauce and lemon juice. Small amount of soft brown sugar. Mix and taste. If it's too sour, add more sugar, if it's too sweet, add more lemon juice.

FISH AND VEGETABLE STEW

This is a 'waste not, want not' recipe following a meal of whole salmon.

Add whatever you've got in the cupboard, garden or the freezer – put the ones which need the longest cooking time in first to save cooking time. I've listed them in the order in which I would add them.

2 cups stock from a whole salmon (boil up bones and skin)

400g tin crushed tomatoes, or fresh tomatoes if your crop is bountiful.

potatoes, diced

carrots

onion

celery, including leaves

green beans

capsicum

corn

peas

400g tin beans

silver beet

grated daikon or English radish

preserved lemon

seasonings of choice

Simmer until it's all cooked (20 – 30 minutes).

Sprinkle fresh herbs and grated parmesan on top and serve with plain bread.

Annette Milligan

$1399
WIN

ROAST SUMMER TURBOT

with Charles Griffin's Nobbled Spuds

I love the succulent sweet softness of turbot. It's one of our most delicious local fish, and even more so when teamed up with crunchy roast spuds. If turbot isn't in, you could use tarakihi or blue cod. Agria spuds are best as they have that great yellow colour, excellent flavor and 'nobble' really well. (Serves 4)

700g turbot fillets, roe removed

6 Tbsp of Nelson olive oil

1kg Agria spuds (or other floury potatoes)

3-4 sprigs of rosemary

half a dozen cloves of garlic

sea salt and freshly ground black pepper

3 tsp of capers

a good handful of vine ripened cherry tomatoes (chopped in half, unless tiny)

1-2 lemons (juice and zest)

Turn oven on to a high setting, ready for the spuds to go in first. Peel potatoes, cut into nice chunks (not too small), put them in a large pot, just covered with water and bring to a rolling boil for about ten minutes. You don't want them to fall apart, but they should have a softness on the outside. Drain in a colander and put them back in the same pot and allow them to dry off for a minute. Then put a top on the pot and give it a good shake. The spuds should have roughened up all over – my granddad Charles was a great roaster of spuds and showed me this trick when I was a kid. When they cook it gives them a fantastic crunchiness.

Hiff the spuds into a roasting dish, give them a good slurp of Nelson olive oil and get them into the oven. You will add rosemary, garlic and salt later. They should take about 40 – 50 minutes to become golden and crunchy.

While the spuds are doing their thing get the fish ready. I like to check the turbot fillets to make sure there are no sneaky scales floating round, and to cut away any bits of roe that are often attached (you can ask for it without the roe). Cut the fillets into two or three depending on the size of the fillet.

Around now chuck some sprigs of rosemary, cloves of garlic and a sprinkling of flaky salt onto the spuds.

Using another roasting pan, put in about 3 Tbsp of olive oil, and the juice of a lemon (zest the lemon first). Coat both sides of each fillet in the oil and lemon juice mixture and arrange them around the pan. You might need two lemons depending on how big they are as it's important that there is a bit of liquid floating round. Sprinkle the capers and the wee tomatoes over the fish and scatter round the lemon zest. Give it all another splash of olive oil, a quick grind of pepper and a sprinkle of flaky Marlborough salt.

It's important that you time all this with serving time in mind. Remember that the spuds will take about 45 minutes but the fish will only take about 6 – 8 minutes to cook. Don't overcook the fish, if in doubt take it out and let it sit under a bit of foil for a couple of minutes and it'll keep cooking.

Serve the fish onto heated plates with some of the accompanying caper and tomato juice spooned over, and let everyone help themselves to the spuds.

You could serve a nice peppery rocket salad as well but to be honest the fish and the spuds are a fabulous match on their own. A nicely chilled Riesling never goes amiss though.

Pete Rainey

Charles Griffin with grandson Pete Rainey.

Turbot prior to roasting.

SMOKED FISH AND KUMARA PIE

Comfort food for a chilly day. Based on an Annabel Langbein recipe this quick pie will warm you all up from the inside out. We go to Guyton's fresh fish shop for the fish. They sometimes have cheaper smoked fish pie pieces, which turns this into an affordable family meal. It is one of the few meals we sometimes eat with a pile of peas which makes it feel like good old fashioned hearty fare. I think you can be pretty loose with the measurements and I sometimes squeeze in lemon juice and chopped parsley. Also delicious with a spinach and orange salad. Serves 4-5.

2 medium kumara

2 potatoes

450g smoked fish, flaked, (or drained and flaked, canned smoked fish)

1½ cups grated, tasty cheese

5 Tbsp butter

1 large onion, finely sliced

¼ cup flour

3 cups milk

½ tsp nutmeg

salt and ground pepper

Optional: 2 cups cooked rice and ¼ cup capers

Cook the kumara and potato in boiling salted water for about 15 minutes until tender.

To make sauce, melt the butter in a heavy based saucepan. Cook the onion for 5 minutes until soft. Stir in the flour and cook for one minute. Gradually add milk, stirring continuously. Season with nutmeg, salt and pepper. Cook, stirring constantly until sauce thickens and comes to the boil. Stir in the flaked fish and rice and capers if wanted. Place the mixture in a greased, medium ovenproof dish.

Drain kumara and potato and mash with a little milk, seasoning to taste with salt and pepper. Spread over the fish mixture. Sprinkle the cheese over the topping. (Dish can be prepared ahead to this point.)

Bake at 220°C for 15-20 minutes until golden brown, or cover and microwave on high for 5 minutes then place under a grill to brown.

Marchant Family

GREEK FISH

I can't remember where this recipe came from but it's one of those great quick to prepare dinners that everyone in our family likes.

olive oil to grease the dish

500g white fish fillets (e.g. tarakihi, snapper, gurnard)

1 large red onion, sliced thinly

handful of fresh oregano, or about 1 tsp of dried oregano

4 Tbsp lemon juice

2 Tbsp olive oil

4 Tbsp fresh parsley

2 large tomatoes, peeled, deseeded and diced

½ cup feta cheese, crumbled.

Lightly oil an oven dish, then place the fish fillets in the bottom. Layer the rest of the ingredients over the top in the order given.

Cook at 190°C for 25-30 min.

This is really nice with a salad and bread rolls or baked potatoes.

Jenny Smith

Biography OF A LOCAL PALATE

In 1944 my father Fred Burton, after being invalided back from the war, began working three days a week at the Hotel Nelson Milk Bar, on the ground floor of a classic Art Deco Hotel that used to stand on the site now occupied by the Museum, on the corner of Trafalgar and Hardy Streets. At the time the Hotel Nelson was the poshest hostelry in Nelson, where the Queen came to stay. Eventually he became a partner in the milk bar, and as a sideline, began doing catering. Within no time the catering snowballed and the milk bar became the sideline, and eventually the Burton Catering Co. had a combined full- and part-time staff of 66.

The 1950s was an ideal era in which to be Nelson's only serious quality caterer. There were debutante balls, put on by the Masons, Nelson College Old Boys and various other service clubs, at which the teenaged daughters of Nelson's bourgeoisie would mimic their counterparts in the English upper class, and don ball gowns and gloves which came up to their elbows. There were huge parishioners' dinners for several hundred, put on by both the Anglicans and the Presbyterians. There were Nelson Ski Club and Chamber Music Society functions, conferences, a great many weddings, and private parties put on in the big houses of Nelson's elite.

Of necessity Fred was self-taught, because in the 1950s there was nobody around to teach him. He built up a library of cookbooks, which lined the pelmet of our kitchen – *Esquires Handbooks for Hosts*, the original big colour-format *Time Life Picture Cookbook*, the grand gilded tomes of collected recipes from Gourmet magazine, witty works on food and wine by Norman Douglas, Stephen Lister and Alex Waugh – books I read and frequently browsed, and which eventually must have influenced me to write my own.

Nowhere was the growing demand for more sophisticated food better reflected than in the post-

war 'smokos' Fred put on for the Nelson RSA. As Fred pointed out in an interview with the Nelson Evening Mail in 1957, the RSA contained the most varied cross-section of the public in one organisation. At first he had provided the traditional food they required, such as pies, saveloys and pigs' trotters. One year, however, the RSA gave Fred a free hand, and he provided 'whole hams, a large range of hors d'oeuvres and other items I thought might be suitable. The platters were swept clean. Not a thing left. Since then they have been willing to try almost anything new and seem to enjoy it.'

Fred was always prepared to push the limits. Despite the import restrictions of the 1950s, he managed to serve tinned French snails, Perigord truffles and frogs' legs at weddings, debutante balls and conference gatherings. For one conference in 1957 he devised a Davy Crockett menu, and very possibly for the first and last time in New Zealand, delegates dined on whale steaks, fresh from Tory Channel. There were also stuffed and roasted quail, an 18-pound snapper garnished and served whole, rabbit pie, venison, wild pork, clams, and that innovation of the 1950s, corn on the cob (sweet corn appears in no New Zealand cookery book prior to 1940, despite maize having been introduced early in the nineteenth century).

During the 1954 Royal Visit to Nelson Fred provided food for the Queen's 'conversazione'. But the two dozen sandwiches supplied for Her Majesty's afternoon tea, in her apartment, caused some raised eyebrows when the bill came to four pounds ten shillings. 'The best quality Russian caviar cost me three pounds ten shillings and the pate de fois gras, one pound,' he explained. The bread and his labour he had supplied at his own expense.

For the visit of Italy's Corelli string orchestra in 1960, Fred baked a pie of ham, veal and egg in the shape of a violin, having had a pie dish custom-made for the purpose. He drew up, in Italian, a menu including grissini, antipasto, Brodo di bue con vermicelli (beef broth with vermicelli), Bistecche di vitello alla graticola (veal steaks cooked on the spot), and one of his signature dishes, creamed scallops in the shell, titled for the occasion, Conchiglie di pesce in creama alla 'Burtoni.'

Fred had befriended Italian soldiers he'd captured in the North African desert, and after the war the Neapolitan tomato growers around Nelson, such as Gugliemo Monopoli. Perhaps these Italians supplied him with the seedlings for the eggplants and capsicums he used to grow in our home garden (and preserve in Agee jars), since neither of these vegetables was then commercially available. At one stage he experimented with making his own salami.

He had a cookshop, that he called his catering depot, in a converted cottage in Cox's Lane. He hired chefs, but also cooked, and one of my early memories is of watching Fred and his team pull steaming suckling pigs out of boiling cauldrons – a blanching process prior to roasting which, along with basting, helped ensure lovely burnished reddish brown skins with crackling. This he regarded as a trade secret, so when a satisfied wedding guest asked my mother if Fred would show her how he cooked his suckling pig, and she, not understanding this, said, 'Yes, of course', it was under distinctly grumpy sufferance that he allowed the woman to invade his inner sanctum for a lesson.

He had very classical tastes which were expressed in the grand, highly decorated buffets he used to present at wedding receptions, in the Baroque curlicues he piped over the suckling pigs, and the glazed apples he stuck in their gobs. Fred was never happier than at the end of a piping bag, which he squeezed with his right hand, guiding the nozzle with the thumb and little finger of his left hand – all that had escaped being blown off when a shell exploded in the breech of a howitzer in 1941 in North Africa.

Royal Visit Dinner

HOTEL NELSON

JANUARY 16th 1954

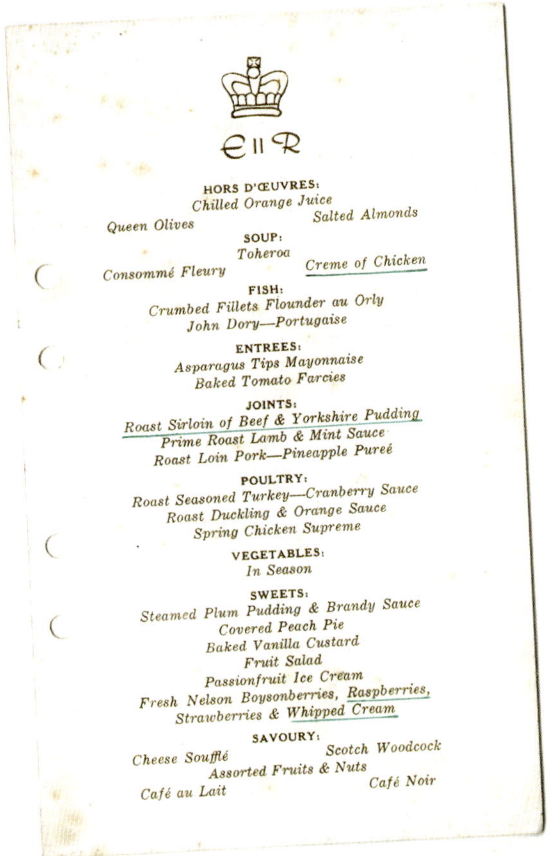

E II R

HORS D'ŒUVRES:
Chilled Orange Juice
Queen Olives *Salted Almonds*

SOUP:
Toheroa
Consommé Fleury *Creme of Chicken*

FISH:
Crumbed Fillets Flounder au Orly
John Dory—Portugaise

ENTREES:
Asparagus Tips Mayonnaise
Baked Tomato Farcies

JOINTS:
Roast Sirloin of Beef & Yorkshire Pudding
Prime Roast Lamb & Mint Sauce
Roast Loin Pork—Pineapple Pureé

POULTRY:
Roast Seasoned Turkey—Cranberry Sauce
Roast Duckling & Orange Sauce
Spring Chicken Supreme

VEGETABLES:
In Season

SWEETS:
Steamed Plum Pudding & Brandy Sauce
Covered Peach Pie
Baked Vanilla Custard
Fruit Salad
Passionfruit Ice Cream
Fresh Nelson Boysonberries, Raspberries, Strawberries & Whipped Cream

SAVOURY:
Cheese Soufflé *Scotch Woodcock*
Assorted Fruits & Nuts
Café au Lait *Café Noir*

Like every other business in 1950s New Zealand, the Hotel Nelson Milk Bar shut on a Sunday, and sometimes Fred would take us children there after hours, and feed us dishes from the menu. My favourite was cold crayfish served with mayonnaise Fred would make with a special gadget, a container that would drip the oil into a bowl in which you would crank a handle to beat it into the egg yolks.

Unlike tearooms, which were a British inheritance, the first New Zealand milk bars had appeared in the 1930s as a result of American influence (and having begun in the United States in the 1920s as a necessary response to Prohibition). Like the classic American milk bar, familiar to most New Zealanders through Hollywood films, the most important feature of my father's Art Deco-style milk bar was the bar itself, which stretched for the entire length of the establishment and curved around a corner, its crowning glory a long strip of pink neon.

Leafing through a book of handwritten recipes he used for the milk bar, I'm amazed at what had to be made from scratch: fruit conserves were boiled with sugar syrup to concoct sundae toppings; fruit salad was made with fresh seasonal fruit, preserved in Agee jars on the premises; and even milkshake flavourings had to be made by mixing concentrates with sugar syrups.

The sundaes, served in thick split glasses with a bright pink triangular wafer and a long spoon, were Art Deco statements in themselves, but by the end of the fifties my father sensed they were dated, and seized the opportunity to run with the new British and American trend, and open the first coffee house in Nelson.

So, in 1958 out came the Art Deco bar, and in came Burton's Coffee House, with pot plants and red striped awning over the stone counter, upon which Fred's staff now served Cona coffee topped with whipped cream. Along the windows facing the street and the intersection, Fred installed a thin counter and high stools, so patrons could watch the street life as they sipped. And each lunchtime he made a point of frying bacon, with the air extractor fan on full blast to the street, to lure punters in by their noses.

Fred never lived long enough to enjoy the coffee house boom of the 1960s, as he died of cancer in 1961, aged 54.

In that same year Eelco Boswijk, a young Dutch immigrant, the son of a psychiatrist from Utrecht set up the Chez Eelco coffee house in upper Trafalgar Street, achieving everything Fred had set out to do, only better. The black ceiling, the Chianti bottles in their woven baskets, the plaited garlic by the servery, the angular cane chairs, the lamp stands of Easter Island heads – all created a stir, but none so much as the giant beaten-copper beetles and insects on the walls, made by Titirangi artist David Kennedy (who later found fame and fortune in Greece), and which now grace the back wall of Eelco Boswijk junior's fine pub, The Free House, in Collingwood Street.

The Chez Eelco survived for decades, becoming a Nelson institution, before finally closing its doors in 2001 after Eelco retired. By then coffee houses, or cafés as we now know them, had become ubiquitous, and drinking good coffee, a national pastime.

David Burton

From *Biography of a Local Palate,*
Four Winds Press, 2003

David Burton was born and educated in Nelson and is a prominent New Zealand food writer. He is the author of numerous books and is currently a senior features writer for Cuisine, *and restaurant critic for both* Cuisine *and* The Dominion Post.

The Boulder Bank

KEDGEREE

Kedgeree is a classic dish that evolved during the Raj, the period from 1858 to 1947 when the British ruled India. Originally a breakfast dish, I think it makes a much better lunch or dinner, and is a big favourite in our family. This recipe is based on one from my brother-in-law David Burton's book *Raj at Table: A Culinary History of the British in India*. It is best eaten warm, not piping hot. You can use more or less curry powder, depending on your tastes. Serves 4.

350g smoked fish fillets (bones removed)
oil
1 large onion, chopped
1 tsp curry powder
1 small tsp turmeric
1 cup long-grained rice
2-3 eggs, hardboiled
1 Tbsp butter
salt and pepper
chopped parsley to garnish
lemon

Cover the fish with boiling water and simmer gently over low heat for 10 minutes. Drain, and reserve water.

Heat a little oil in bottom of heavy saucepan and fry chopped onion until transparent. Then add rice, curry powder and turmeric and stir until rice is lightly glazed.

Measure 2 cups of reserved fish water (making up the amount with extra water if necessary) and add it to the rice and onion. Cover the pot tightly and cook for about 14 minutes or until all the liquid has been absorbed by the rice.

Meanwhile, break up the fish into flakes, and hard boil the eggs.

Add the fish flakes into the rice mixture, and season to taste with salt and pepper. The eggs can either be chopped and added to the rice at this point, or quartered and placed on the side at serving. Use parsley and a wedge of lemon to garnish.

Kedgeree is especially nice if some cream is poured on just before serving. Lois Daish also recommends dark-frying extra onion rings as an additional garnish, which I often do.

Susannah Roddick

Sweet Treats

the Suter Café

We have both done a lot of eating and travelling and agree that Nelson allows us to have our cake and eat it too. We saw that the location of The Suter was perfect but the café needed a lift. Being great optimists we believe that our rejuvenation of the café has restored vitality to it. The changing environment at the Suter Gallery and the seamless surroundings of the Queen's Gardens is really the icing on the cake.

Numero Uno at the Suter Café is our Orange Almond Cake. Moroccan originally, then via Claudia Roden, this recipe came to us from Pandoro Bakery in Auckland. We both adore Middle Eastern flavours: the gorgeous Katrina, thanks to her upbringing and Nicky from early discoveries in Sydney, and later setting up a groovy little Casbah 'Mecca' in Hong Kong.

Nicky Cantrick

Orange Almond Cake

This recipe uses oranges but tangelos are a beautiful alternative.

The Slushy (Make at least a day in advance and chill until required)

3 oranges

Cover the oranges in water, bring to the boil, then drain. Cover the cooked oranges with fresh water and boil for 1 hour. Drain, cool and then process to a rough slushy consistency. Refrigerate. This keeps for up to two weeks.

The Cake

8 eggs

2 cups sugar

3½ cups ground almonds

1½ cups orange slushy

1 tsp baking powder

Preheat oven to 170˚C and line a 30cm round cake tin with baking paper.

Whisk together eggs and sugar until thick and the volume has doubled. Add slushy. Fold in almonds and baking powder. Pour into prepared cake tin and bake for 1 hour, turning the tin once.

The Dressing

6 Tbsp smooth apricot jam

100g toasted sliced almonds

Melt the jam until runny, then stir in almonds and spread evenly over the cake. Leave to set somewhere cool before attempting to cut.

I make a large quantity for two cakes at the café but have halved the recipe here. It makes a lovely modern low cake in a 30cm cake tin. A smaller tin could be used but it would need to be cooked for longer, and carefully at a lower heat.

This cake keeps wonderfully refrigerated.

Nicky Cantrick and Katrina Kalill

Painting by Nicky Cantrick

Classic Banana Cake

This classic cake recipe is taken from the 1948 Nelson Central Home and School Association cookery book. The recipe recommends 'this cake may either be iced with lemon icing or covered with mashed bananas and whipped cream'.

4 oz butter (115g)
1 small cup sugar
1 egg
1½ breakfast cups flour
1 tsp baking powder
2 or 3 bananas, mashed
1 tsp baking soda, dissolved in 2 Tbsp milk
vanilla essence

Cream butter and sugar, add egg and beat well. Add mashed bananas.

Mix flour and baking powder together, add to mixture and then essence, beat well.

Lastly, add soda dissolved in milk.

Cook in moderate oven (180°C) for 35 minutes.

Margaret Martin (1948)

Carrot Cake

This carrot cake recipe comes from a friend who lives in Australia. She would use a cup of oil, 2 cups sugar and fewer spices, making it slightly soggy in texture as a dessert. This recipe presents as a moist, easy to cut cake. Over the years it has gone down well at Nelson Central School cake stalls. It would be cut up and sold by the slice. For galas, I would often triple everything (except oil which I doubled) and cook in a roasting dish. This took 1½ - 1hr 40mins to cook.

All the family enjoys receiving carrot cake for birthdays. I almost always freeze it in advance and ice it on the day. I passed this recipe on to my mother many years ago. She regularly bakes this recipe to give out to the sick and bereaved within her community and if you ever visit her she always has one in her freezer to pull out and offer with a cuppa.

Cake
1 cup wholemeal flour
1 cup plain flour
2 tsp baking soda
1¼ cups raw sugar
¼ tsp salt
2 tsp cinnamon and 2 tsp mixed spice
½ cup cooking oil
4 eggs, beaten
3 cups grated carrot

Icing
100g cream cheese
50g butter
1 tsp vanilla essence
2 cups sifted icing sugar
1 cup chopped nuts (optional, either mixed into icing sugar or sprinkled on top)

Preheat oven to 180°C.

Sift and mix dry ingredients. Add oil and stir well. Stir in beaten eggs and carrot.

Mix thoroughly. Grease the sides of 10" (25cm) square or round cake tin and line bottom with baking paper. Pour mixture into prepared tin.

Bake for 1 hour or until cooked.

When cold, ice with icing made by beating all ingredients together thoroughly, or ice with lemon icing. It is also fine without any icing.

Kaye Mount

Gateaux

Cooking *for Radio*

Once upon a time there was no television in New Zealand. During the 1950s and early 60s radio was a major source of information and entertainment. Station 2XN was Nelson's call sign. My responsibility was Women's Hour which broadcast between 9 and 10am. This kept me busy, collecting commercials to ad lib and sourcing programmes to interest women, who were usually housebound with small children and no car. Many programmes featured food. I remember two occasions well, the first a traditional Christmas Pudding which would be worthy to grace the table of Charles Dickens, the second was a demonstration of a brand new product which would revolutionise a woman's work in the kitchen – the Instant Pudding!

To give the Christmas Pudding recipe an unusual edge, Cerys, a marvellous Welsh cook, and I decided to make it in situ rather than in the studio. This was a very novel idea in those days and the session was recorded in her 'storybook' cob cottage kitchen in Nayland Road, in the area where Kidson Construction is now. The kitchen had a marvellous atmosphere with a wood range, herbs drying from hooks in the ceiling, and a well-scrubbed wooden table for us to work on. All ingredients ready, huge pot on the range, recorder switched on, we then described the making of the pud. We made four puddings in the traditional round style, which we put in cloth and lowered into the pot to boil away merrily for four hours. Returning the next day to collect two of the puddings, Cerys told me they had to 'dry out'. I did this by hanging them on the clothesline, then into the cupboard to wait until Christmas. The recipe became very popular and many copies were stencilled and mailed out. Why didn't the cyber age come earlier?

My second memory is the live demonstration of the Instant Pudding. Remember this was the era of steamed puddings, tapioca, rice, fruit pies and tarts so when this pudding came on the market it was a sensation! All you needed was a packet of instant pudding and a pint of milk (only one variety delivered by the milkman – full cream milk) plus a jar of cherries to decorate. The broadcast was going very well. The women were suitably impressed by the ease of making the pud, which looked very good with the cherry on top and so I naturally asked the women to partake – I can still see the look on their faces – in my haste I had grabbed a jar of red cocktail onions!

Sylvia Monk, in her role as Women's Reporter for Radio 2XN, presenting the title 'Mrs New Zealand Nelson' to Barbara Leov, in 1962 and then parading through town.

Christmas Pudding

(original measurements converted to metric)

115g plain flour
115g breadcrumbs (fresh)
226g suet (shredded)
226g demerara or brown sugar
1kg mixed fruit and peel
4 eggs
½ tsp nutmeg
2 tsp mixed spice
1 tsp salt
1 cooking apple peeled and grated
1 orange, rind and juice
2-6 Tbsp brandy

Well grease the basin (or basins, if you prefer smaller puddings) and put a pot of water on to boil for each basin.

Sift dry ingredients together. Add all other ingredients. Mix thoroughly to a soft mixture and tip into basin/s, filling to within 20mm of top. Grease a large round of greaseproof paper for each basin, cut a piece of foil to same size. Put both rounds together, foil uppermost, fold across centre to form a 2cm pleat and lay over basins with greaseproof side next to mixture. Tie down securely with string.

Lower into boiling water and keep topping up for 4 hours. When cooked, lift basins out carefully, leave foil and greaseproof paper on puddings until cold before re-tying with freshly greased paper and foil and store in a dry cupboard.

(If you want to boil in cloth, flour first and then make a ball and put in cloth, tying tightly and then lower into water. When cooked dry out and then store.)

Cerys and I had a load of fun and although traditional Christmas puddings are not so popular I still make them (in a pudding basin not cloth). In fact there is one in the cupboard all ready for Christmas 2012.

Sylvia Monk (now Wesney)

Last dip! Tahunanui Beach

Chocolate Zucchini Cake

We call this 'chocolate cake' when friends come over as the children are initially put off by the zucchini. But once they taste it they love it. It is a parent's way of getting some green vegetables into their children!

125g butter
1 cup brown sugar
½ cup white sugar
3 eggs
1 tsp vanilla essence
½ cup yoghurt
2½ cups flour
¼ cup cocoa
2 tsp baking soda
1 tsp cinnamon
½ tsp mixed spice
1 tsp baking powder
3 cups grated zucchini
1 tsp salt

Line square pan with baking paper.

Beat butter and sugar until light and creamy.

Add eggs (one at a time) with one spoonful of flour.

Add vanilla essence and yoghurt, mix well.

Sift all dry ingredients and partly combine with butter mixture.

Add zucchini, don't over mix. Turn into pan.

Bake at 170ºC for about 45 minutes.

Harriet Denham

'I queue alongside a gaggle of ravenous ex-pat Germans to buy the nation's best bratwurst from Doris's German small-goods stall. I stock up on fresh chorizo from George, the lovely Portuguese guy, and cadge a few morsels of his sherry-roasted pork.'

Grant Smithies

Gingerbread Cake

This reminds me of gingerbread my grandmother would make for me as a child and now it is one of our family favourites. It never fails to impress and is oh so very easy to make! This keeps really well...that's if you can hide it away in a tin from the family! The original recipe is from *The Perfect Cookbook* by David Herbert, but I have changed the quantities to make a lighter cake and reduced the amount of sugar syrup to pour over the top.

60g butter, cubed
125g golden syrup (6 small Tbsp)
95g plain flour (generous ½ cup)
30g self-raising flour (¼ cup) or use plain flour with ¼ tsp baking powder
1 tsp bicarbonate of soda
1 heaped tsp ground ginger
½ tsp mixed spice
100g caster sugar (⅓ cup)
pinch of salt
125ml milk
1 egg, beaten
Syrup:
40g sugar (3 Tbsp)
40ml water
1 Tbsp very finely grated fresh ginger

Preheat the oven to 170°C. Thoroughly grease a 23 x 12cm loaf tin and line the base with baking paper. Put the butter and golden syrup in a small saucepan. Melt, stirring occasionally, over a low heat, then remove from the heat. Sift both flours, the soda and the spices into a mixing bowl. Stir in the sugar and salt, then add the milk and egg, and mix until smooth. Gradually add the melted-butter mixture, stirring until well incorporated. Pour the batter into the loaf tin and bake for 40 minutes, or until risen and firm to the touch. A skewer inserted into the middle of the cake should come out clean. Allow the cake to cool in the tin for 5 minutes before turning out onto a wire rack to cool. Make a syrup by placing sugar, water and grated ginger in a small saucepan. Bring it to the boil and simmer for 5 minutes. Spoon syrup over the hot cake and leave to cool.

Victoria and Thomas Goode

Speedy Lemon Cake

This is a good cake for a gala or when you need something quickly as you don't need to ice it. Always a winner!

1½ cups flour
1 cup sugar
1 tsp baking powder
¼ tsp salt
125g butter
2 beaten eggs
½ cup milk
rind of 1 lemon

Grease and line a ring tin. Turn oven to 180°C

Mix the first 4 ingredients together in a large bowl. Cut or rub in butter until the texture is like breadcrumbs, then stir in remaining ingredients.

Pour into prepared tin and cook 40 minutes.

Meanwhile combine the juice of the lemon with ¼ cup of sugar. When cake is cooked remove from oven and immediately pour juice and sugar mixture over. Leave to cool before serving.

Kristin Tilley-Brown

Purple Cake Day

kids helping kids all over the world!

Cupcakes, kids, creativity and compassion all come together on Purple Cake Day, and Nelson Central School has been involved since it launched on the 1st of March, 2011.

Purple Cake Day celebrates children, and empowers them to learn about children globally and fundraise for those in need. This year Central School joined many other schools and communities in 18 countries around the world who dressed in purple, sang purple songs, created purple art and made, ate or sold purple food.

Driven locally and growing globally, the charity was established by Nelson woman Emily Sanson-Rejouis in the spirit of her two beautiful daughters, Kofie and Zenzie, who tragically died with their father in the massive Haiti earthquake in 2010. From an early age Kofie reached out to children living on the street, wanting to share her things with them. Zenzie, when asked by Emily what she wanted for her 4th birthday, said 'A purple cake, two purple cakes!' Sadly, that was a week before the earthquake and Zenzie did not live to celebrate her birthday. But the spirit of her daughters and their compassion and childish creativity, inspired Emily to launch a movement to celebrate and connect children all over the world and encourage action for those in need.

Every year a new 'country in focus' is chosen and a resource kit with loads of creative ideas and superb education resources is made available freely to schools online at: www.purplecakeday.org. Children, families, teachers and communities around the world are getting on board - celebrating, learning, connecting and making a difference for children in need. It's easy and fun to get involved in Purple Cake Day - start with this simple and delicious cupcake recipe and go wild with purple icing. Visit the website for more information, recipes and ideas.

Emily Sanson-Rejouis

Quick and Yummy Cupcakes

Everyone can have fun making cupcakes for Purple Cake Day. Here is a great recipe for kids to mix up themselves! Makes 12 cupcakes.

125ml oil or melted butter (about 125g or ½ cup solid butter)

1 cup self-raising flour (or plain flour with a tsp baking powder) sifted

½ cup sugar

pinch of salt

2 eggs (beaten)

1 tsp vanilla essence

¼ cup milk

purple cake day® .org

Preheat oven to 180°C. Mix all ingredients in a bowl until just combined. Spoon into paper cupcake cases. Bake for 12 - 15 minutes. **Optional:** Stir in ½ cup frozen blueberries before baking.

Go Wild with Purple Icing! Making purple icing can be challenging. You can buy red and blue food colouring and try making your own or use natural purple colouring. Here are a few ideas...

Make a basic butter icing, or use cream cheese or icing sugar and mix with any of these:

Blueberry pulp, tamarillo juice, beetroot juice, boysenberry pulp. Or go to your local organics store and see if you can find purple carrot colouring.

An easy alternative is to buy ready made white icing (fondant) and add a touch of purple gel colouring, usually sold at cake decorating and party shops. Add fantasy and fun with purple sprinkles, sugar flowers and stripy candles.

Moist Fruit Cake

My mother's favourite and apparently also popular with her visitors, as she calls it her "Cut and Come Again Cake". Keeps well.

10 oz (300g) plain flour
1 tsp baking powder
pinch of salt
1¾ lb (470g) mixed dried fruit (currants, raisins, sultanas)
8 oz (220g) butter
2 eggs
8 oz (220g) soft brown sugar
½ large can evaporated milk

In a bowl, sieve flour, baking powder, salt and then stir in fruit.

Cream butter and sugar in a separate bowl.

Add beaten eggs gradually to the creamed mixture.

Fold in fruit and flour alternately with evaporated milk.

Bake in a greased 8" (20cm) tin at 150°C for 1¾ hours.

Kathryn Robertson

Black's Sponge

This sponge recipe was given to Robert Black, pastry cook and baker of Black's Bakery in Gloucester Street, by Hugh Blanchfield, a fellow baker in the 1960s.

Robert used the recipe for many family celebrations and the sponges he made were legendary in the family for their 'height and lightness'. Hugh told him 'you can't over-beat a sponge. Treat it very gently and with respect when folding in the flour. You need to keep the air in the mix.'

This recipe can be halved to make a single sponge.

Delicious with cream and jam, fresh berries or other local seasonal fruit.

6 eggs (at room temperature)
6 oz sugar (171g)
3 oz high grade flour (85g)
3 oz maize (not wheat) cornflour (85g)
2 tsp baking powder
½ tsp vanilla (optional)

Lightly grease two round sandwich tins (23 cm approx) and dust with flour.

Warm a large mixing bowl with warm, not hot, water and then dry.

Add eggs and sugar, then beat until the sugar is dissolved and the mixture is light and fluffy...'it can never be over beaten'. Add vanilla. Sieve flour, cornflour and baking powder.

With a wooden spoon, gently fold in small quantities of the flour into the egg mixture.

When all the dry ingredients are mixed in, gently pour the sponge into the two prepared tins and bake at 190°C for about 20 minutes.

Cool in the tins for 20 minutes, then run a knife around the edge and the sponge should come free. Transfer to a cooling rack.

Fill the cooled sponge with preferred fillings.

Top with a dusting of icing sugar.

Best eaten on the day!

Brenda Black

Frances Rae's father, who was also a legendary sponge maker, recommended dropping the sponge, from knee height onto the floor when removing from the oven, to prevent sagging!

GRIFFIN AND SONS

The Griffin's Factory

Many older Nelsonians will remember the warm sweet smells from the Griffin and Sons' factory wafting over the city. It is such a strong memory for me that I can still smell it. The daily five o'clock punctuation of the Griffin's steam whistle, signalling the end of another shift, was woven into our lives.

Filling the site diagonally opposite Nelson Central School, the Griffin's factory was the source of wonderment for generations of Nelson school kids, and after 1938 when the biscuit production shifted to a new factory in Lower Hutt, the Nelson factory was even more tantalising, as it produced sweets only. Those sweets, such as wine gums, chocolate fish, pineapple lumps and Pinky bars were staples for generations of New Zealanders.

For me the memories of Griffin's are more powerful than for most. John Griffin who started the business in 1855 was my great great grandfather. He sailed to New Zealand from the Isle of Wight with his wife and children in 1854, and set up a bakery business in Trafalgar Street. A series of factories were built on the Alton Street site over the years, with interruptions from some catastrophic fires, while the final brick factory was built in 1903. That factory closed in 1987 and was demolished soon after. Some of the original buildings still remain on the site.

My grandfather Charles (John's grandson) was managing director of the company for many years right up until Griffin and Sons Ltd was sold to the National Biscuit Company of America in the early 1960s. Charles was quite a character, and my brothers and I loved visiting our grandparent's house to seek out the big cartons of wine gums fresh from the factory. He would entertain us with competitions to see who could peel the longest unbroken apple peel, and showed us how to make whistles out of green willow sticks. Any visit would be marked by a cup of tea and a piece of my grandmother May's Chinese Chew.

Pete Rainey

Pictures above: John Griffin and the Griffin's Factory in the background. Picture taken from Shelbourne Street.

May Griffin's Chinese Chew

- 1 egg
- ¾ cup sugar
- 2 cups mixed fruit (raisins, sultanas, dried apricots, craisins etc)
- 1 cup flour
- 1 tsp baking powder
- 125g butter melted with
- 1 Tbsp golden syrup

Preheat the oven to 180°C

Cream the egg and sugar. Add in the mixed fruit, flour and baking powder and mix well.

Melt the butter and golden syrup and add into the mixture. Mix well then turn the mixture out into a greased slice tin. Then into the oven for about 25 minutes but don't overcook. Cut while warm. Allow it to cool and then dust with icing sugar.

Always serve with a cup of tea - preferably in a large china teacup.

Nana Pat's Cookies

From my 84 year old Nana Pat, who says this is her best and most requested recipe ever. Also very easy for children to make.

100g butter
4 oz sugar (½ cup)
1 egg
1 pinch salt
1 tsp vanilla essence
6 oz flour (1 cup)
1 tsp baking powder
1 Tbsp cocoa
1 cup sultanas
walnuts if desired

Cream butter and sugar until fluffy. Add beaten egg, then vanilla essence. Fold in sifted dry ingredients alternately with sultanas. Roll teaspoon sized balls and press with a fork onto baking paper lined oven trays.

Bake at 180°C for about 12-15 minutes.

When cool, ice with chocolate icing and dip into coconut.

Lee-Anne Weenink

Lottie's Melting Moments

I enjoy baking all kinds of biscuits but this is my absolute favourite. You can flavour the icing with any flavour and for fun, add colouring to the biscuits to match the flavour of the icing. (Mum reckons a teaspoon of ginger in the biscuit mixture goes nicely with lemon icing.) Makes about 16 biscuits.

200g softened butter
¾ cup icing sugar
1 cup flour
1 cup cornflour

Icing
1 cup icing sugar
¼ tsp vanilla essence or another flavour
1 tsp butter
a little boiling water to mix

Preheat the oven to 180°C. Beat butter and icing sugar until light and creamy. Sift flour, cornflour and baking powder into a bowl. Add to creamed mixture. Mix well. Roll dough into small balls (the size of large marbles) and place on oven trays. Flatten slightly with a fork. Bake for 20 minutes. Transfer to wire racks.

When cold, sandwich 2 biscuits together with icing.

To make the icing, put icing sugar, essence and butter in a bowl. Add enough water to mix until spreadable.

Charlotte Halsey

The Maitai River

Like many Nelsonians, the Maitai River has always run through my Nelson summers. As children my siblings and I spent countless hours in and on the banks of the river. Most summer afternoons Mum would take us up the river, where we swam and looked for crawlies, bullies, trout and eels. Just as childhood summers should be, they were deliciously simple times. The sky was always blue; the river clear and clean.

Black Hole, opposite Branford Park, was one of our favourite swimming holes, but we also swam at other popular spots including Denne's Hole, Girlies Hole and Waahi Taakaro, which we called "the wacky-tacks".

Tired and cold from swimming, Mum would feed us her delicious homemade lemon cordial and legendary home baking. Her soft morish gingernuts were a personal favourite.

Growing up we heard stories about how previous generations of Kidsons had visited the Maitai River before us. Dad told us of sometimes skipping school to fly fish in the river. The Kidsons were one of a number of families who built wooden holiday homes in the Upper Maitai Valley. Dad holidayed at "the whare" as a child, negotiating the series of fords in the river to get there. We never visited the whare, and the shaded spot it occupied now lies deep under the waters of the Maitai dam.

We still go up the Maitai and each visit reinforces how lucky Nelsonians are to have such a treasure so close to town.

Sally Kidson

The old Kidson holiday home in the Upper Maitai Valley, now under the waters of the Maitai Dam.

The Kidson family swim in the Maitai River.

Brenda's Lemon Cordial

6 lemons, the zest of 4
8 cups sugar
50g tartaric acid
1 Tbsp epsom salts
6 cups boiling water

Squeeze the lemons and sieve the juice. Put all ingredients in large pot and dissolve the sugar, wait until cool and pour into sterilised bottles.

Brenda Kidson

Brenda's Chocolate Chip Cookies

(originally from Margaret Fay)

500g butter
6 Tbsp sweetened condensed milk
600g flour (2 cups)
400g energy chocolate
200g sugar (1 cup)
few drops of vanilla essence
4 tsp baking powder

Cream butter and sugar. Beat in condensed milk and vanilla. Stir in dry ingredients and chopped chocolate. Roll into golf ball size balls and place on cold tray allowing some room for expansion. Flatten with fork.

Bake 170°C for 20 minutes or 150°C on fan-bake.

Makes three trays of biscuits.

Brenda Kidson

Raspberry Jam

My mum taught me how to make jam when I was ten. This was the first jam I ever made and it's still the one I make most often.

1kg fresh or frozen raspberries
1 lemon, juice
1kg sugar

Cook the raspberries and lemon juice over a low heat for about 10 minutes, until the raspberries are soft. Add the sugar and turn up the heat, stirring until all the sugar has dissolved (about 5 min). Boil rapidly for about 5 minutes, until you reach a set (when you put some jam on a cold saucer, the surface should wrinkle when you push your finger through it). Take off the heat and stir every now and then for about 10-15 minutes (this stops all the seeds from floating to the top of the jar) and then pour into hot jars. Cover with a lid or cellophane covers. Makes 2 large jars.

Jenny Smith

Sam's Feijoa Jam

I wanted a recipe for the feijoas from my trees. My grandmother, Anna made up this recipe when she was staying with her mother and the feijoas were dropping everywhere. They don't need to be big fruit as you can scoop out the flesh with a teaspoon. You can make this recipe as big as you want by increasing the quantities. This makes two small jars of jam. It is quite low in sugar, so it might need to be kept in the fridge.

2 cups of chopped fruit
1 cup of sugar

Mix sugar with fruit and leave for a while.. an hour or up to 2 days, until juice from fruit runs into the sugar.

If you like more zing you can add sliced crystalised ginger or a small quantity of finely sliced lemon or mandarin.

Boil gently for about 20 minutes, turn off element and leave until jam sets when dropped onto a cold saucer. Pour into sterilised jars.

This recipe also works well with kiwifruit and guavas (but you need to mouli the guaras to get rid of the stones).

Sam Halsey

Kirkpatrick's Jam

As a young child I remember going up Vanguard Street and smelling the sweet, rich smell of fresh jam from the Kirkpatrick's factory. My grandparents lived up the road and had both worked there; they retired when the factory closed. Granddad made the tea, morning and afternoon in huge watering can-like teapots, one with a 'T' welded on it, which he gave to my brother. I am now the keeper of the pots and proudly have them, although not to pour tea, but as a decoration.

The factory had been operating since the 1890s. It was set up by Samuel Kirkpatrick to utilise the region's ability to produce quality fruit and berries, which would otherwise be difficult to transport to market elsewhere in the country. Kirkpatrick's was a major employer, especially of women, in Nelson. Pulping, canning and jam making continued until the factory closed. The site is now occupied by a New World supermarket, which among other products does sell jam, just not 'K' Jam!

Dene Gornall

Strawberry Jam

1kg strawberries
1.5kg sugar
1 heaped tsp tartaric acid

Hull the strawberries and place the fruit and sugar in pan.

Stir until boiling and boil hard for 3 minutes.

Add the tartaric acid and boil for another 5 minutes without stirring.

Allow the mixture to become almost cold before bottling to prevent fruit rising to the top.

Pour into sterilised jars.

"K" Jam, Miss Bush, fancy dress. The Nelson Provincial Museum, Tyree Studio Collection: 62826

Rocky Mallow

This is Isla's dad's favourite childhood recipe. It was lost for many years and after many attempts to recreate it from memory, we gave up. Then one day, going through his mother's old recipe books, a slip of paper fell out and on it this handwritten recipe (his mother's original!). So now we have had it a million times, or so, since. Making up for lost years. The marshmallow is very high so make sure your tin has generous sides! Lining the tin with a big piece of baking paper right up the sides is helpful.

Base

150g butter (melted)
2½ weetbix (crushed)
1 cup flour
1 cup dessicated coconut
¾ cup sugar
2 Tbsp cocoa
1 tsp baking powder

Pour the melted butter over the dry ingredients and mix well.

Press into a 23cm (9 inch) tin and bake for 15 minutes at 180°C

Marshmallow

Dissolve 2 dessertspoons of gelatine in 1 cup of boiling water.

Add 2 cups of sugar and a few drops of vanilla essence.

Beat until thick and fluffy and pour over the cooked base while still in tin.

Sprinkle with coconut and allow to set before cutting.

Katy and Marc Kerby

Gingernuts

100g butter
1 Tbsp golden syrup
1 cup sugar
1 egg
1¾ cups flour
2 tsp ginger
1 tsp baking soda

Preheat oven to 190°C.

Melt butter in saucepan. Stir in syrup and remove from heat. Add sugar and egg and beat with wooden spoon. Sieve in dry ingredients and mix. Spoon warm mixture onto greased oven tray and allow room for spreading, or form balls when cool and place on tray.

Reduce heat and bake at 180°C for 10 minutes.

Chocolate Weetbix Slice

This is a great treat to make and uses up any broken weetbix. Always better the day after you have made it as the icing soaks into the weetbix and makes the slice really moist.

150g butter, melted
4 weetbix (crushed)
½ cup sugar
1 cup flour
1 Tbsp cocoa
1 tsp baking powder
a few drops vanilla essence

Mix all dry ingredients in a bowl, making a well. Then add melted butter and vanilla essence. Mix together, then press into a slice tin. Bake at 180°C for 10 minutes. Make icing while baking.

Icing
1½ cups icing sugar
1 tsp cocoa
hot water to mix (add a dollop of butter for a creamier icing)

Mix all icing ingredients and spread over slice while hot. Cut into squares when almost cool.

Victoria and Thomas Goode

Almond Biscuits

Crisp and delicate and fast to make, especially in a food processor.

100g soft butter
½ cup sugar
1 cup flour
1 tsp baking powder
½ tsp almond essence (optional)
¼ - ½ cup toasted slivered almonds

Cream butter and sugar. Add remaining ingredients and mix. Add milk if too dry. Form into a cylinder and chill. When cold, cut into thin slices. Bake on greased oven tray at 170°C for 10 minutes.

Eat-Me-Quicks

In 1975 Margareta and I made the risky decision that I would earn my living as a writer. We arrived in Nelson and for several years were church-mouse poor, so buying cheap food was a necessity. We soon discovered that the area was rich in things that grow and that pick-your-own lowered costs even further. We picked peas in Appleby, strawberries, raspberries and boysenberries at Richmond, and best of all, apples at an orchard at the head of Eves Valley, starting with early season varieties and going right through to Granny Smiths at the end. There's nothing better than ripe apples, straight from the tree, we always had a box full in the wash house. Our favourites were Golden Delicious, a variety hard to find now. A bonus at Eves Valley was that mushrooms grew in the paddocks next to the orchard. A friend gave us a beer recipe and for several years we brewed our own, as well as ginger beer until the bottles started exploding.

So we got by, things improved, and Margareta was able to buy real coffee instead of drinking a make-believe sort made from roasted barley. But we never lost the pick-your-own habit, which became even more useful when one of our daughters (both were at Central School) went through a vegetarian phase. Fresh fruit and vegetables became even more important. As for puddings, which children must have, apple crumble and golden syrup pudding were cheap and easy to make, but best of all were Eat-Me-Quicks. We still have the recipe, handwritten on a stained old catalogue card.

Maurice Gee

Base

- 2 cups flour
- 2 tsp baking powder
- ½ tsp salt
- 1 ounce butter (25g)
- ⅔ cup milk
- 2 apples
- 1 cup sultanas
- 2 Tbsp sugar

Syrup

- 1 Tbsp golden syrup
- 1 ounce melted butter (25g)
- 1 cup hot water

Sift the flour, baking powder and salt into a bowl. Cut in butter and mix to a soft dough with milk. Roll the dough out into an oblong. Combine peeled and thinly sliced apples with sultanas and sugar and scatter over the dough. Roll up from the long side and cut into 1 inch slices. Put into a greased baking dish. Combine golden syrup, melted butter and hot water and pour over the slices.

Bake at 220°C for 15 minutes. Serve hot.

Maurice Gee on his seat beside the Maitai River

Flapjacks

This is a firm family favourite. We grew up in England and these were always in our lunchboxes. I learnt the recipe from my mother and have been making them ever since for my family.

225g margarine
225g demerara sugar (1¼ cups)
2 Tbsp golden syrup (I prefer Tate and Lyle brand)
275g rolled oats (2¾ cups)

Pre heat oven to 160°C.

Melt margarine in a large pan with sugar and syrup on a low heat and stir.

Once combined and melted add the oats and mix well. Make sure they're all covered with liquid. Press flat into a roasting tin (that is greased or lined with baking paper).

Bake for about 35 minutes, until pale golden brown.

Leave to cool in the tin for 10 minutes, then mark into squares and leave until completely cool before removing.

Julia Cooke

Cinnamon Rolls

This is a fantastic recipe and everyone is guaranteed to enjoy the results. Just making these rolls makes you feel good – they fill the house with the wonderful smell of fresh baked bread combined with cinnamon. A great treat for lunch boxes.

Dough
1½ tsp dry yeast
1 cup warm milk
½ cup sugar
½ cup melted butter (100g)
1 tsp salt
2 eggs
4 cups plain flour

Filling
1 cup brown sugar
2½ Tbsp cinnamon
⅓ cup very soft butter (75g)
½ cup raisins (optional)

Dissolve yeast in half the milk with 1 tsp of the sugar until frothy. Combine all the dough ingredients and mix until it forms a smooth ball. Cover with a damp kitchen towel and let rise until double in size, about 1 hour. Punch the dough down and roll out to a 55cm x 40cm rectangle, ½ cm thick. Brush with softened butter and sprinkle with brown sugar, cinnamon and raisins. Roll up the dough lengthwise and cut into 16 slices. Place rolls, swirly side up, on two large greased baking trays. Cover and let rise for 30 – 60 minutes. Bake at 170°C for approx.20 minutes – until golden on top.

Suzanne Thompson

Katie Pascoe uses almost the same dough for her Blueberry Breakfast Brioche, but doubles all the ingredients, except the sugar (both recipes use ½ cup sugar). Her dough is rolled out thicker (about 2.5 cm) and as the name implies, she replaces the spicy filling with blueberry jam and 1¼ cups of blueberries, sprinkling brown sugar over the buns before baking.

LAVENDER FROM NELSON

Muffin Mix

This mixture can be used to make any flavour of muffins, sweet or savoury and so it is great for using up seasonal windfalls of fruit or excess vegetables.

For sweet base

2 eggs

2 cups milk

200g melted butter

4 cups self raising flour (or plain flour with 4 tsp baking powder added)

1 cup sugar

optional: substitute 2 cups of flour with 2 cups of bran

For savoury base

2 eggs

2 cups milk

150g melted butter

4 cups of self raising flour

½ cup sugar

2 cups cheese

Mix wet and dry ingredients separately. Add fruit, vegetables, herbs etc to wet ingredients.

Add dry ingredients and fold in until just mixed. Do not over mix.

Pour mixture into greased or lined muffin tins.

Bake at 180°C for 15 minutes and a further 15 minutes at 150°C.

Mandy and Laura Joy

Baked Fruit

Very easy and always delicious. Apricots and plums are best, but most fruit is nice.

Put fresh fruit, halved or whole in a baking dish with minimal water. Cover with vanilla sugar. Cook in a very slow oven for about an hour, until fruit is wrinkled and soft. Serve with whipped cream and a muffin, cake or a slice.

Melrose House

Melrose House was built in 1879 for Englishman Charles Watts, who came to Nelson as a seventeen year old in 1841. He was an employee of the New Zealand Company, working as an Improver (survey cadet) and in the early 1840s was involved in surveying the Brook, Maitai and Takaka Valleys. In January, 1844 he was part of a successful expedition to find an alternative route from Nelson to the Wairau Valley, via Pelorus. Charles Watts married Elizabeth Nixon and they had seven children. Watts died in July 1881 and later that year Watts' daughter Frances married prominent local lawyer Percy Bolland Adams and their son Percy, a lover of trees and the outdoors, developed the stunning gardens around Melrose.

Melrose was left to Percy, and after his wife Eileen became involved with the Women's Division of Federated Farmers the house was gifted in 1944, to be used as a home where countrywomen could rest and recuperate. In 1973 the WDDF relinquished the house due to high running costs and ongoing maintenance but made provision that the house be held for the benefit of the citizens of Nelson.

Nelson City Council at first declined the gift of the house feeling that it would be a burden to ratepayers. What followed were months of debate through public meetings, petitions, submissions and newspaper articles. In February 1974, the uncertainty over Melrose's future lead to the auctioning of all furniture and fittings, right down to the brass knocker on the front door. Later that year concerned members of the public formed the Melrose Society, agreeing to maintain responsibility for the daily running of the house on behalf of the council, including a live-in caretaker.

Melrose House is now used as a majestic venue for weddings, birthday celebrations, high teas, business meetings and family gatherings. With the recent renovations and stunning redecoration, the house is now a 'must see' attraction for both visitors and locals. The recent opening of Melrose House Café makes the house more accessible to all. Those who wish to take in the history over a lovely light lunch or cup of tea can enjoy being part of this grand building's rich life.

Angela Kernohan

Strawberry Tiramisu

250ml strong coffee
4 Tbsp Cointreau
2 punnets of strawberries
4 egg yolks
½ cup sugar
¼ cup Cointreau
¼ cup water
250g mascarpone
250ml cream
1-2 packs savoiardi thins (sponge fingers)

Mix the coffee with 2 Tbsp of the Cointreau. Hull the strawberries and slice thinly, sprinkle over the remaining Cointreau and set aside.

Beat the yolks until light and fluffy.

Meanwhile, heat the sugar, ¼ cup of Cointreau and the water in a small saucepan. Stir until the sugar has dissolved, and bring to the boil. Boil for 1 minute.

Add the syrup to the yolks in a slow steady stream, beating continuously. Continue beating until the mixture has thickened and cooled. Add the mascarpone and cream and beat until the mixture thickens. (Be careful not to over mix as the cream might curdle.)

To assemble: layer the ingredients in glasses or in one deep bowl. Gently dip the thins in the coffee mix, count 2 seconds then pull them out. (If left too long, they will go soggy and make the Tiramisu too wet. If not soaked long enough, the Tiramisu will remain hard.)

Layer the thins, then cream mixture, then strawberries until each glass is full – the last layer being cream.

Chill in the fridge for 2 hours, then serve.

This will last up to 4 days, and does taste better the next day!

Angela Kernohan (Melrose House Café)

Berry Water Ice

Perfect for excess ripe berries. Try red currants with raspberries and add lemon-scented geranium leaves to blackberries. Delicious with something creamy.

500g ripe, sieved berries
½ cup sugar
600ml water

Boil sugar and water for 5-6 minutes. When cool, add syrup to sieved berries. Freeze for 2½ hours.

Anna Adams

NILE ST

Fruit Foraging

Apples are Nelson's star fruit for me, so I love that this spicy pudding cake is almost more apple than sponge. My mum used to bake it for us when we were greedy teenagers (I've no idea where she found the recipe - possibly an old Woman's Weekly). It makes a big, yummy, moist cake that's wonderful warm with custard but just as delicious the next day in your lunchbox. Though I haven't tried it, I reckon pears would be just as good in it and maybe even feijoas or a mixture. Both are plentiful in our region. Nelson's fruitful abundance, in particular the amount of "free" food that can be foraged from here, has been my most exciting discovery since moving back home last year. Whoever came up with the Open Orchards initiative deserves a prize. When plants are needed, it just makes so much sense to plant edibles. Because of the project, beautiful big fig and walnut trees can be found up the Maitai, plums and strawberries flourish along the paths where I walk my dogs, and yesterday I found out there's a banana tree in Bridge Street! To see where all the Open Orchard plantings are, you can check out the Google map at www.transitionnelson.org.nz. I'm keeping an eye on the heritage apple trees around the corner from my house in Stoke to go into a batch or two of these wedges.

Sally Butters

Food Editor, *NZ House & Garden Magazine*

Apple Wedges

125g butter, softened
2 cups sugar
4 eggs
2 cups flour
1 tsp baking powder
½ tsp baking soda
1 tsp each: ground nutmeg, cinnamon and ginger
pinch of ground cloves
pinch of salt
6 cups sliced apples (about 6-7 apples)

Cream butter and sugar. Add eggs and beat well. Sift in dry ingredients and blend well. Lastly mix in apples. (Don't chop them too small or the cake will be soggy - I just slice them randomly into chunks.)

This mixture fills a small meat dish. It can be halved successfully.

Cook at 180°C for 1 hour.

SPECIALS
OPEN TILL 6pm
EGGPLANT $2.00
BEANS $2.00 BAG
CAPPI TOMS $4.00kg
CUCUMBERS $1.00
RASP
STRAW
BOYSEN
BLUE
BERRIES
CUSTOMER PARKING
pause...
refreshes you right

Crêpes à la Française

250g flour
3 eggs
500ml milk
6 tsp caster sugar
1 tsp oil
pinch of salt
30g butter (for cooking)
Optional: a tsp of rum, Amaretto or Grand Marnier

Pour the flour into a dish and gradually add the milk, the eggs, the sugar, the salt and the oil and optional rum, Amaretto or Grand Marnier. Mix well with a whisk to avoid lumps. Heat a non-stick pan and grease with butter.

Pour a half-ladle of the crepe batter and cook 1-2 minutes per side.

Eat with icing or brown sugar, honey, or even better, with vanilla icecream, whipped cream, chocolate syrup or golden syrup.

Tastes great with seasonal fruit such as freshly picked berries, stewed stone fruit or poached autumn fruit.

Anne Rousseau

Super Pikelets

Nana Henderson is not our nana, but the nana of one of our friends. This is her recipe and it makes the fluffiest, yummiest pikelets ever.

1½ cups flour
pinch of salt
1 tsp cream of tartar
1 tsp baking soda
1 large Tbsp butter
1 large Tbsp golden syrup
1 egg
1 cup milk

Sift flour, salt, baking soda, and cream of tartar together. Melt butter, golden syrup, and sugar and allow to cool. Beat egg well and add to butter mixture, add milk and flour alternately to egg/butter mixture, adding a little more milk if necessary to reach the right consistency. Cook in spoonfuls in a pan over a medium heat.

Jenny Smith

Emma's Moreish Meringues

These perfect little (or big if you want) meringues go fabulously with a variety of tasty additions. Chocolate sauce, berries, fruit, ice cream and yoghurt have all been known to accompany this wonderful treat but they also taste just as amazing by themselves, especially if you don't have the desire to do another load of dishes! It is recommended that you double the recipe when baking for a large crowd, children's birthday parties or your supposed '29' year old friend's birthday party.

3 egg whites (at room temperature)
½ tsp vinegar
pinch salt
1 cup sugar
¼ tsp vanilla

Preheat oven to 130-150°C. Add vinegar, salt and vanilla to whites and beat mixture until it forms peaks. Add sugar gradually and keep beating until it is very stiff and glossy.

Put spoonfuls on an oven tray. Bake for 45 minutes.

Emma Halsey

Waffles

I have made waffles for many kindy galas, school camps and Nelson Central School galas when my children were there. Although waffles originate in Belgium, this recipe is the way my grandma in Holland used to make them.

She had a big cast iron waffle iron that she cooked on the gas stove. I use a modern waffle maker. Not weight watcher's friendly but oh so lekker (yummy).

900g flour
500g butter
8 eggs
500g sugar
water

Cream butter and sugar. Add the eggs one by one until you get a creamy mixture.

Add the flour. Not all at once.

You can leave it thick or add some water if you prefer a thinner mixture (you will get more waffles this way).

Bake your waffles until golden in a waffle maker. This batch should make 28 waffles.

Sprinkle icing sugar over the top. Whipped cream and fruit makes a delicious treat.

Eet smakelijk.

Yvon Smits

Luscious Lemon Tart

This is one of Nana Mary's best recipes. It is easier in a food processor but can certainly be made without one.

Base

125g butter, softened

1 cup flour

½ cup icing sugar

Filling

1 cup caster sugar

½ cup lemon juice

grated rind of 2 lemons

2 Tbsp custard powder

½ tsp baking powder

3 eggs

icing sugar to dust

To make the base, place butter, flour and icing sugar in food processor. Run machine until pastry clumps together in ball around blade.

With floured hands press mixture into base and up sides of greased flan dish.

Refrigerate for at least 30 minutes. Sets firm but bakes best from being cold.

Preheat oven to 180°C

Place all filling ingredients into cleaned processor and run until well combined.

Pour into chilled base.

Bake 25 mins or until pastry is crisp and golden and filling set.

Dust with icing sugar to serve.

Lee-Anne Weenink

Nymph's Kiss Panna Cotta

1 vanilla pod

1½ cups cream

1 lemon, peeled rind

¼ cup sugar

2 tsp gelatine

2 Tbsp Nymph's Kiss honey liqueur (from Snapp Dragon Distillers, Golden Bay or the Nelson Market)

or ¼ cup Amaretto

¾ cup cream

Bring first measure of cream to boil with the vanilla, lemon rind and the sugar. Once it has boiled remove from the heat and strain.

Sprinkle gelatine over the Nymph's Kiss honey liqueur and microwave until all the gelatine granules have dissolved. Then pour the gelatine mixture into the hot cream. Put into fridge and let it semi-set, stirring occasionally so as to not let the mixture form a skin.

Whip remainder of cream, and then fold in the mixture from fridge. Pour into 6 x ¾ cup moulds, refrigerate for 4 hours. Once Panna Cotta has set remove from its moulds and serve.

Angela Kernohan (Melrose House Café)

MORRISON café STREET

It started in a little cottage in Morrison Street with bacon and eggs served with hollandaise and pesto, a soft sweet lemon slice and smooth, beautifully-made coffee. Fifteen years later these items are still on the menu and Morrison Street Café is now one of Nelson's iconic cafés, having built a reputation over the years for its coffee, food and service.

But a lot has happened along the way. In 1997 owner, Kay Field, saw a gap in the market. 'Nobody was doing good espresso then.' But when she talked of opening somewhere that did she was told repeatedly that Nelson didn't need another café. She opened one anyway and has never looked back. The menu was simple, with breakfast and cabinet food. 'It was tiny inside, so we started doing catering as well to cover for wet days when no one could sit outside.'

A year later the fan base had grown and Kay's brother, Scott, of Wilkins and Field asked her to join him in a café-garden centre development as part of the Mitre 10 complex across the street. So in 1998 the café moved to its current location in the historic Morrison and Sclanders building on Hardy Street, where the café could open directly into a sheltered garden centre courtyard. Ten years later Mitre 10 moved out of the central city and the café became part of the Fashion Island retail complex. The garden courtyard was replaced with a sunny terrace.

In 1995, as part of a major rebranding, the move was made to table service and the menu has since developed a reputation for healthy natural flavours and a good range of allergy-free dishes. Today the bacon and eggs and the lemon slice are just part of a much larger menu and a good cup of coffee is as important as ever.

Sue Farley

Chocolate and Berry Brownie

450g butter, softened
3 cups sugar
2 tsp vanilla essence
6 eggs
½ cup rice flour
240g cocoa (about 2 cups)
pinch of salt
3 cups mixed berries, fresh or frozen (chopped if large)

Cream butter and sugar until white and creamy. Add vanilla essence and eggs, mixing in one at a time. Gradually add dry ingredients mixing gently. Add the berries and mix.

Pour and spread evenly into a swiss roll tin lined with baking paper.

Bake at 180°C for 40 minutes, or until skewer comes out clean.

Ganache Icing

250g dark chocolate

100g sour cream (warmed in microwave)

Melt chocolate in the microwave in 40 second bursts until melted (or in a bowl over a pot of boiling water). Add warmed sour cream and whisk together until smooth.

Chocolate Cheesecake

This recipe seems complicated, but really isn't. It is totally worth the effort for any special occasion. Dedicated to Chris Allen, who loves it every time. We think this cheesecake is delicious served with fresh Nelson berries.

For the base

125g digestive biscuits

60g butter (melted)

1 Tbsp cocoa

For the filling

175g dark chocolate, chopped

500g cream cheese

150g caster sugar

1 Tbsp custard powder

3 large eggs

3 large egg yolks

150ml sour cream

½ tsp cocoa, dissolved in 1 Tbsp hot water

For the glaze

75g dark chocolate, chopped

125ml cream

1 tsp golden syrup

Preheat oven to 180°C

To make the base: Crush biscuits to make rough crumbs (you can use a food processor), then add butter and cocoa. Process until damp clumps form and then press evenly into a 23cm springform cake tin. Place in freezer while you make the filling.

To make the filling: Melt chocolate, either carefully in microwave or in a bowl over boiling water. Set aside to cool slightly. Beat the cream cheese to soften it and then add the sugar and custard powder and beat to combine. Beat in the whole eggs and then the extra yolks and the sour cream. Finally, add the cocoa dissolved in hot water and melted chocolate, mixing to a smooth batter.

Take the tin out of freezer and cover the outside of the cake tin with a good layer of plastic wrap and another layer of strong foil over that, to protect the cheesecake in the water bath.

Sit the cake tin in a roasting pan and pour cheesecake filling into the cake tin. Then fill the roasting pan with boiling water to halfway up the cake tin.

Bake 45-60 minutes (the top should be set but the underneath should still wobble).

Peel away the foil and plastic wrap.

Leave to cool in tin on a rack, then into fridge, covered, to set overnight.

Return to room temperature, before un-springing from tin.

To make glaze: Gently melt chocolate, cream and syrup. Remove from heat and whisk to a smooth sauce. Drizzle over cheesecake and save any excess as a serving sauce.

Jasmine, Ollie and Jacob Patel (from Nigella Lawson's Feast*)*

BAKERS FLOUR
gilmours
BAKERS
FLOUR
Net Weight 20kg

Lemon Flummery

This recipe is one of my mother's favourite 'special' dessert recipes. She would make it for special occasions, serving it either in a large crystal bowl or in individual parfait glasses. In Nelson it is a very cheap dessert to make because of our ability to grow lemons. I grew up in Invercargill and although Mum tried to grow a lemon tree in a sheltered spot for years, she had no success and so she had to buy lemons. It can be made on the stove or in a microwave.

1 cup plus 2 Tbsp of water
1½ Tbsp butter
2 lemons, rind and juice
4 Tbsp plain flour (use a metric spoon)
½ cup sugar
2 eggs, separated

Stove method:

Boil water, butter and grated lemon rind. Mix flour and sugar and whisk into liquid. Then whisk egg yolks into mixture.

Bring slowly to the boil. Simmer 10 minutes. Stir constantly.

Add juice and cool. Fold in well-beaten egg whites.

Pour into serving dishes and refrigerate.

Microwave method:

Add a little of the water to the flour, mix and then add the remaining water.

Melt the butter and add with the sugar and egg yolks. Mix well.

Microwave on high for 2 minutes. Stir, and microwave for another minute or two. Mix well, and if necessary microwave some more as if you are making custard.

Add lemon juice and mix well and cool. Then fold in well-beaten egg whites.

Pour into serving dishes and refrigerate.

Frances Rae

The 'Mud Flats', Atawhai

Local Fruit Crumble

I know crumble is nothing new but other than Paul's fantastic Sunday morning pancakes, this Nigel Slater recipe is a regular in our household. We love this crumble as it's really easy, all measurements are approximate, it requires no pre-cooking of the fruit and keeps well. Siobhan loves it for breakfast.

Filling

about 1kg raw fruit, roughly chopped into even sized pieces:

apple (peeled) and boysenberry or plum (stoned and quartered) or feijoa

50g sugar, white or brown (optional: you may prefer more sour fruit)

spices as desired

Topping

150g plain flour

100g butter, hard from the fridge

75g castor or light brown sugar

optional: a handful of rolled oats

Filling

Spread the fruit in an oven dish and flatten slightly. Then stir in the sugar to mix.

Add any spices you like, such as cinnamon with apple.

Topping

Blend flour and butter in food processor or by hand, until it looks like breadcrumbs.

Add sugar and oats and blend quickly until mixed in. Spread over top of fruit to cover.

Bake for 30 to 40 mins at 190°C until fruit is cooked and the top has lightly browned.

Ali Howard, Paul and Siobhan Jonkers

Green Tea Custard

Desserts don't feature large on Japanese menus and they are usually small, simple and light.

Make an egg custard, flavour it with powdered green tea (macha tea).

Pour into glasses to set.

Top with some red berries, or a red berry coulis, sauce or puree.

If you want to be really fancy you can add a blob of whipped cream and some grated chocolate on top.

Annette Milligan

Cinnamon Sugar Baked Walnuts

We were given these walnuts as a present from one of our neighbours at our housewarming, and housewarming this treat sure was! They taste absolutely divine.

1 egg white
2 cups walnuts
1 cup sugar
2 Tbsp cinnamon

Beat egg white until stiff (like meringues). Add walnuts and mix well.

Stir in sugar and cinnamon until well blended. Place on a flat oven tray covered with baking paper, in small dollops.

Bake at 220°C for 10 – 15 minutes or until they look like meringues. Let cool completely.

Store in an air tight container or jar.

Chantel Cameron

Belgian Chocolate Truffles

250g dark chocolate (at least 70% cocoa)
125g unsalted butter
2 egg yolks
10g vanilla sugar
125g icing sugar
50g cocoa
2 tsp rum or Amaretto (optional)

Break the chocolate into little pieces in a dish and let it melt in a bain marie (water bath).

Add chopped butter gradually. Mix.

When the butter has melted well in the chocolate, remove the dish from the bain marie and add the egg yolks, the vanilla sugar and the icing sugar and the optional rum or Amaretto. Mix well.

Put the dough in the refrigerator for at least one hour so that it solidifies.

Then, with your hands, form small balls, roll them in the cocoa, then arrange them on a dish.

Anne Rousseau

INDEX